Guilty as Sin

GUILTY

AS

SIN

UNCOVERING NEW EVIDENCE OF CORRUPTION AND HOW
HILLARY CLINTON AND THE DEMOCRATS DERAILED THE FBI
INVESTIGATION

EDWARD KLEIN

REGNERY
PUBLISHING
A Division of Salem Media Group

Regnery® is a registered trademark of Salem Communications Holding Corporation

Cataloging-in-Publication data on file with the Library of Congress

ISBN 978-1-62157-641-9

Published in the United States by
Regnery Publishing
A Division of Salem Media Group
300 New Jersey Ave NW
Washington, DC 20001
www.Regnery.com

Manufactured in the United States of America

10 9 8 7 6 5 4 3 2 1

Books are available in quantity for promotional or premium use. For information on discounts and terms, please visit our website: www. Regnery.com.

Distributed to the trade by
Perseus Distribution
250 West 57th Street
New York, NY 10107

ALSO BY EDWARD KLEIN

NONFICTION

All Too Human:
The Love Story of Jack and Jackie Kennedy

Just Jackie:
Her Private Years

The Kennedy Curse:
Why Tragedy Has Haunted America's First Family for 150 Years

Farewell, Jackie: A Portrait of Her Final Days

The Truth about Hillary:
What She Knew, When She Knew It,
and How Far She'll Go to Become President

Katie:
The Real Story

Ted Kennedy:
The Dream That Never Died

The Amateur:
Barack Obama in the White House

Blood Feud:
The Clintons vs. the Obamas

Unlikeable:
The Problem with Hillary

NOVELS

If Israel Lost the War
(With Robert Littell and Richard Z. Chesnoff)

The Parachutists

The Obama Identity
(With John LeBoutillier)

ANTHOLOGIES

About Men
(With Don Erickson)

For D.J.B. Forever

CONTENTS

PROLOGUE

Rigged

The Executive Terminal at Phoenix Sky Harbor International Airport
Monday, June 27, 2016

Bill Clinton's private jet was cleared for takeoff and was taxiing toward the active runway when a Secret Service agent informed him that Attorney General Loretta Lynch's plane was coming in for a landing.

"Don't take off!" Bill barked.

As his plane skidded to a halt and then headed back to its parking space, Bill grabbed a phone and called an old friend— one of his most trusted legal advisers.

"Bill said, 'I want to bushwhack Loretta,'" the adviser recalled in an interview for this book.* "'I'm going to board her plane. What do you think?' And I said, 'There's no downside for you, but she's going to take a pounding if she's crazy enough to let you on her plane.'

"He knew it would be a huge embarrassment to Loretta when people found out that she had talked to the husband of a woman—the presumptive nominee of the Democratic Party—who was under criminal investigation by the FBI," the adviser continued. "But he didn't give a damn. He wanted to intimidate Loretta and discredit [FBI Director James] Comey's investigation of Hillary's emails, which was giving Hillary's campaign agita."

Bill hung up the phone and turned to a Secret Service agent.

"As soon as her plane lands," he said, "get the attorney general on the phone and say the president would like to have a word with her."

Several minutes later, Loretta Lynch came on an encrypted phone line.

Lynch owed the former president big time. Seventeen years before, he had appointed her U.S. attorney for the Eastern District of New York, one of the highest profile prosecutorial posts in the country. Now, the man who had made her career was on the phone inviting himself to visit her on her plane, and Lynch couldn't bring herself to say no.

Bill walked across the seventy-five yards that separated his plane from hers. It was 108 degrees in Phoenix, and Bill later recalled that he could feel the heat through the soles of his shoes.

---

* The source, who has been close to Bill Clinton for four decades, was interviewed twenty-five times for this book.

Meanwhile, his Secret Service detail and Lynch's uniformed FBI agents were frantically scurrying around her plane, trying to secure the area. They ordered everyone to put away cell phones. No pictures of this meeting would be allowed.

Bill shook hands with Lynch's agents and nodded to the Air Force pilot standing at attention at the bottom of the stairs.

"He told me he bounded up the stairs of her plane on pure adrenalin," Bill's adviser said. "It brought out the old fighter in him. During Hillary's campaign, he'd been feeling weak; he didn't have the fire in his belly. But his fury over the FBI witch-hunt of his wife, whom he loves with a passion despite all the shit he gets up to—that infuriated him. You can say anything you want about him, and he'll let it go. But attack his wife, and he'll try to destroy you."

Once inside Lynch's plane, Bill turned on the Clinton charm. He gave Lynch's shoulder an affectionate squeeze and shook hands with her husband, Stephen Hargrove.

"Bill said he could tell that Loretta knew from the get-go that she'd made a huge mistake," his adviser said. "She was literally trembling, shaking with nervousness. Her husband tried to comfort her; he kept patting her hand and rubbing her back.

"Bill made small talk about golf and grandchildren and [former Attorney General] Janet Reno, and he kept at it for nearly a half hour. It didn't make any difference what they talked about; all he wanted to do was send a message to everyone at Justice and the FBI that Hillary had the full weight of the Clinton machine, the Democratic Party, and the White House behind her.

"It was clearly tortuous for Loretta. Bill told me later that he noticed there were beads of sweat on her upper lip.

"Like all attorneys general, Loretta is accustomed to being treated as royalty wherever she goes, but here she was sitting in her plane, entirely helpless, being intimidated by this wickedly clever old coyote, who had bushwhacked her on the Arizona desert."

Aspen Ideas Festival, Aspen, Colorado
Friday, July 1, 2016

On the final day of the Aspen Institute's annual summer get-together for self-congratulating liberal elites, Jonathan Capehart, a member of the *Washington Post* editorial board and an MSNBC contributor, interviewed Attorney General Loretta Lynch.

It was four days since the airport encounter between Lynch and Bill Clinton, and in the public furor that ensued, everyone—Democrats and Republicans alike—agreed that the meeting had seriously compromised the FBI's investigation into Hillary's use of an unsecure private email system when she was secretary of state.

Capehart and Lynch sat on a raised stage, a few feet apart—the thin, wiry journalist dressed incongruously in a dark wintry suit; the attorney general in a black dress, pink jacket, and a double strand of pearls.

"You have a reputation of having the highest integrity, utmost, solid judgment," Capehart began. "…A lot of people were like… friends, supporters, backers, are saying, 'What on earth was she thinking?' talking to Bill Clinton?"

"Well, I think that's the question of the day, isn't it?" Lynch replied, visibly squirming in her chair. "…Certainly my meeting with him raises questions and concerns, and so, believe me, I completely get the question...."

She then launched into a long explanation of the process.

"...So back to my first question," Capehart pressed Lynch. "The what-were-you-thinking question."

Lynch giggled nervously, but didn't reply.

"But let me put a different spin on it, and ask," Capehart continued. "When you're on your plane...and knowing how the protocol works...you're on your plane and in walks the former president of the United States. What were you thinking?"

After some back and forth, a crescendo of laughter rose from the audience as Capehart—pretending to be Lynch talking to Clinton—said, "'Get off my plane! What are you doing here?'"

Lynch laughed along with the audience in an effort to hide her humiliation.

"That team [career Justice Department agents and investigators, reviewed by the FBI] will make findings...," she said earlier in the conversation, "and I fully expect to accept their recommendations."

With those words, she effectively recused herself from the case. But Capehart wasn't satisfied.

"Do you regret not telling the former president of the United States to leave the premises?" he asked. "...And so of course, what's happened as a result of this, there are people out there in the world who are saying, 'See, this is an example of the system that's rigged against the rest of us.'"

Meet the Press
Sunday, July 3, 2016

> **Andrea Mitchell:** I was told that there was a possible plan
> for [Hillary] to fly in on Tuesday with…Obama [for a
> campaign appearance] to North Carolina on Air Force
> One, the full embrace, the picture.
>
> **Chuck Todd:** So Hillary Clinton would have been on Air
> Force One with Obama, walking down.
>
> **Mitchell:** No, coming out of the—
>
> **Todd:** Off the—
>
> **Mitchell:** —the door of the plane opens, there are two of
> them, arm in arm.
>
> **Todd (sounding incredulous):** Not now [in the midst of the
> FBI investigation]!
>
> **Mitchell (explaining):** …It really makes it hard for the
> president while [the FBI investigation of Hillary] is
> pending from his Justice Department.

Interview with a source close to presidential consigliere
Valerie Jarrett*
Monday, July 4, 2016

"Obama wouldn't have invited Hillary to fly with him to
North Carolina and let her use two of the greatest symbols of
presidential power—Air Force One and the podium with the seal
of the president of the United States—if he thought there was even
the slightest chance she was going to be indicted. But Loretta

---

* The source, who has known Valerie Jarrett since her undergraduate days at
Stanford University, was interviewed twelve times for this book.

Lynch had been assuring him and Valerie for weeks that the prosecutors at Justice would never let that happen, and that the fix was in.

"A lot of people thought Jim Comey didn't give a shit about the prosecutors at Justice or the political fallout, that he was hell-bent on indicting Hillary, that he was the Eliot Ness of his time—squeaky clean and untouchable.

"But that was a complete misreading of Comey, who's a complicated guy. Yeah, he comes across as a straight arrow, but you don't get to be director of the FBI by falling off the turnip truck. It takes huge drive and ambition and an instinct for political survival. And Comey knew that if he recommended an indictment of Hillary—something that was fiercely opposed by the president, the attorney general, the Democrats in Congress, and the liberal media—if he did that, he'd ignite a firestorm and go down in history as the man who traumatized the country's political system. And if, after all of that, Hillary was ultimately found not guilty by a jury, it would blacken Comey's reputation for all time to come."

J. Edgar Hoover Building, Washington, D.C.
11 a.m., Tuesday, July 5, 2016

Dressed in a blue shirt and gold tie, which matched the colors of the FBI flag standing behind his lectern, the dark bags under his eyes masked by TV makeup, James Comey methodically laid out a bill of indictment against Hillary Clinton.

To the press assembled in the FBI auditorium, and the millions watching on TV at home, Comey said that despite Hillary's claim that no classified information had passed through her email system, in fact 110 of the 30,000 emails that Hillary handed over to the State Department contained information that was classified at the time she sent or received them.

He said that "a very small number" bore markings that identified them as classified—another fact at odds with Hillary's frequent statements that none of the emails were marked classified.

He said that Hillary "used her personal email extensively while outside the United States, including sending and receiving work-related emails in the territory of sophisticated adversaries," and that it was therefore "possible that hostile actors gained access to Secretary Clinton's email account."

He said that "there is evidence to support a conclusion that any reasonable person in Secretary Clinton's position...should have known that an unclassified system was no place for that conversation."

He said that Hillary and her top aides at the State Department—Huma Abedin, Cheryl Mills, and Jake Sullivan—had been "extremely careless in their handling of very sensitive, highly classified information."

On and on he went, for a full ten minutes, making an ironclad case that Hillary was guilty of gross negligence in her handling of classified material, and that she had violated a federal statute that did not require evidence of intent to prove her guilty.

The reporters in the room—and the millions watching at home—had every reason to expect that Comey was going to recommend an indictment of Hillary Clinton.

Robert F. Kennedy Department of Justice, Washington, D.C. 11:06 a.m., Tuesday, July 5, 2016

Loretta Lynch certainly thought so.

The attorney general sat in her office, along with her top aides, watching Comey deliver his blistering rebuke of Hillary Clinton.

Lynch had promised President Obama and Valerie Jarrett that Hillary would not be indicted, but here was the director of the FBI on national TV laying out what appeared to be an unassailable case for prosecuting her.

How could this have happened?

What had gone wrong?

Would she be forced to resign?

All these thoughts went through Lynch's mind, as she later recalled to a friend, as she listened to Comey drone on.

She was livid.

Finally, she couldn't stand to watch him anymore.

She covered her eyes with her hands and let out a string of curses aimed at Jim Comey.

J. Edgar Hoover Building, Washington, D.C. 11:14 a.m., Tuesday, July 5, 2016

And then, three quarters of the way through his news conference, Comey dropped a bombshell.

The FBI, he said, would *not* recommend that criminal charges be brought against Hillary for her handling of classified information. There was no evidence, he said, that Hillary had intentionally transmitted or willfully mishandled secret documents in order to harm the United States.

"Our judgment is that no reasonable prosecutor would bring such a case."

The assembled reporters sat in stunned silence.

For months, one conservative commentator after another had predicted that the Democratic president in the White House would never permit his appointed attorney general to go along with a recommendation to indict his party's presumptive presidential nominee. However, there were many liberals, both in and out of the mainstream media, who disagreed with this cynical forecast.

These people had drunk the James Comey Kool-Aid. They had, in the words of the *Wall Street Journal*'s Kimberley A. Strassel, "drooled over" the erstwhile Eliot Ness. They fervently believed Comey would do the right thing. Hillary was clearly guilty as sin, and the right thing would have been for Comey not only to *say* so—which he did—but to make her *pay* for her sins.

But he didn't.

And nothing since the O. J. Simpson not guilty verdict in 1995 left so many Americans doubting the words engraved on the portico of the United States Supreme Court building: Equal Justice Under Law.

The *Wall Street Journal* was blunt. In an editorial headlined "Jim Comey's Clinton Standard" and subtitled "He shows how she broke the law and then rationalizes no indictment," the paper argued:

> The rule of law requires its neutral application. We almost wish Mr. Comey had avoided his self-justifying,

have-it-both-ways statement and said bluntly that he couldn't indict Mrs. Clinton because the country must be spared a Donald Trump Presidency. It would have been more honest and less corrosive to democracy than his Clinton Standard.

Typically, Donald Trump was blunter still:

@realDonald Trump
The system is rigged....

PART 1

HILLARY

The Clinton years might seem like a long national nightmare of scandal, sleaze, and ruthless acquisition of power. Hillary herself is the link from the excesses of the Watergate staff, to the Whitewater fiasco, to abuses of executive power, to the defense of her husband's perjury and obstruction of justice. But now it is Hillary's turn. The Clinton era is far from over and Hillary's ambitions far from satisfied.

—*Hell to Pay*, Barbara Olson

CHAPTER

1

"The Sky Is Falling"

T here were moments—and this was one of them—when Huma Abedin felt more like Hillary Clinton's shrink than her best friend and trusted adviser.

The two women were strapped into the seats of a chartered jet as it touched down at the Bill and Hillary Clinton National Airport on the outskirts of Little Rock on a blistering hot day in July 2015. In a few hours, Hillary was scheduled to deliver the keynote address at the Arkansas Jefferson-Jackson Dinner, and she was in no shape to give a speech.

She was in a rage.

As Huma later described the fit to a colleague who was interviewed for this book, the object of Hillary's rage was James Comey, the director of the Federal Bureau of Investigation. Comey had recently launched a massive probe into Hillary's home brew email system, and it had ignited a media frenzy and put Hillary's bid for the presidency at serious risk.

"It's more right-wing bullshit on top of more right-wing bullshit," Hillary bristled, according to Huma.

Comey, she said, *would end up like all the other Clinton enemies.*

"And how did Bill's impeachment work out for those moth-erfuckers?" Hillary said.

Huma knew better than to contradict Hillary.

But the FBI investigation posed a far greater threat to Hillary than anything she had faced in the past: Troopergate, Paula Jones, Travelgate, Vince Foster, Monica Lewinsky, Juanita Broaddrick, and all the rest. And James Comey wasn't some right-wing nut or clueless prosecutor like Kenneth Starr of Whitewater fame.

Still, Hillary was defiant.

"Let Comey bring it on," she crowed. "Bring the bullshit on!"

———

Hillary's temper tantrums were the stuff of political legend—and said a lot about her character.

"She is so nasty to her Secret Service agents, who would lay down their lives for her," says Ronald Kessler, the author of *The First Family Detail*, "that being assigned to her detail is consid-ered a form of punishment and the worst assignment in the Secret Service."

Her obnoxious behavior was nothing new.

Back in 1974, when Hillary worked for Bernard Nussbaum, a senior member of the House of Representatives Watergate Committee, she blew up after Nussbaum expressed doubts that Hillary's twenty-eight-year-old boyfriend, Bill Clinton, would one day become president.

"She looks at me and says, 'You don't know a goddam thing you're talking about," Nussbaum recalled. "'You're a blank. You're a blank.' She used strong curse words that she uses. She started bawling me out. I mean, she worked for me on the staff, but she was reacting to this. She walks out and slams the door on me."

Hillary has always had the reputation of swearing like a drunken sailor. Here are some choice examples from well-researched books of Hillary's vulgar mouth:

- From *Inside*, by former Secretary of Health, Education and Welfare Joseph Califano: "You sold out, you motherfucker! You sold out!"
- From *Unlimited Access*, by Clinton FBI Agent in Charge Gary Aldrich: "Stay the fuck back, stay the fuck away from me! Don't come within ten yards of me, or else! Just fucking do as I say, okay!"
- From *The Truth about Hillary*, by Edward Klein: "Where's the miserable cocksucker [referring to her husband]?"
- From *Unlikeable*, by Edward Klein: "She freely admits she's always had anger issues," an acquaintance said. "When she's annoyed by people, which is

often, it shows. She's never suffered fools gladly. As
far as she's concerned, politics is all about sucking up
to people she considers beneath her and unworthy of
sharing her space."

According to an oral history of the Clinton presidency conducted by the University of Virginia's Miller Center, Hillary was
impossible to work for in the White House.

"She just let everybody have it," said Leon Panetta, who
served as Bill Clinton's chief of staff. Panetta recalled an aide telling him, "The first lady just tore everybody a new asshole."

Joan Baggett, who served as assistant to President Clinton for
political affairs, said aides were afraid to take on Hillary even
when she was wrong.

"She would blow up over something that she misinterpreted,"
Baggett said. "I remember one time in one of these meetings
where she was blowing up about [Bill Clinton's] staff and how we
were all incompetent and he was having to be the mechanic and
drive the car and do everything that we weren't capable of."

Fast forward to the 2016 presidential campaign, and Hillary
was still at it—still blowing up at the least provocation—which
raised the question whether she had the temperament to be president of the United States.

"She has had screaming, child-like tantrums that have left
staff members in tears and unable to work," one of her campaign
workers told the author in an interview for this book. "People
have walked out from her Brooklyn campaign office and while
they were on the campaign trail with her. At one point recently,

she was berating a low-level campaign worker for making a scheduling mistake. The girl had the nerve to walk away from her, so Hillary grabbed her arm and twisted it. I know that Bill has tried to calm her, but that only makes her more angry."

▬▬▬

Huma had a lot of experience dealing with people like Hillary—vulgar people who thought they could get away with things.

She married such a person—Anthony Weiner, the former congressman whose multiple sexting scandals finally forced her to seek a separation. Before Weiner, there was Huma's father, Syed Zainul Abedin, a Ph.D. from the University of Pennsylvania who was affiliated with the Muslim Brotherhood, a fundamentalist group dedicated to spreading sharia law, which called for the stoning of adulteresses, the flogging of gamblers, and the amputation of thieves' hands, among other things. Huma worked as assistant editor of the magazine, the *Journal of Muslim Minority Affairs*, for thirteen years—from 1995 to 2008—and her mother is still the editor in chief. In a 2002 issue, her mother suggested that the United States deserved to be attacked on 9/11 because of "injustices" heaped upon the Muslim world.

Why Huma was drawn to people like Weiner, or for that matter Hillary, was a question only she could answer. But she put her experience of living and working with such challenging people to good use. She understood what made Hillary Clinton tick, and how to talk her down from the adrenaline high that fueled her bitter, self-pitying rages.

Staffers at Hillary's Brooklyn campaign headquarters said that Huma was closer to Hillary than anyone other than Bill and Chelsea—and that it was a toss-up when it came to Chelsea. Huma's skill managing Hillary was one of the main reasons she had risen from the post of "body woman," general assistant, to the pinnacle of Hillary's presidential campaign, outranked only by two people—campaign chairman John Podesta and manager Robby Mook.

Her cozy relationship with Hillary paid off for Huma in other ways as well. When Hillary was secretary of state, she approved paperwork that permitted Huma to draw a salary of $135,000-a-year as a "special government employee" while Huma freelanced as an independent operator at the Clinton Foundation, where her fluency in Arabic (she grew up in Saudi Arabia) came in handy soliciting donations from Arab governments.

Huma's flagrant conflict of interest didn't stop there. She was also a paid adviser at Teneo, a firm that was founded by a former Bill Clinton operative. Teneo represented clients from the Middle East who conducted business with Hillary at the State Department.

As a result, just three months after the launch of Hillary's presidential campaign, Hillary and Huma were the subjects of two separate but interconnected FBI's investigations—into Hillary's email practices and her suspected pay-to-play corrupt relationship with the Clinton Foundation.

■■■■■

As usual, Hillary blamed her problems on right-wing political conspirators. And for the record, members of her inner circle went along with her paranoid delusion. Privately, however, they conceded that Hillary had a persecution complex, and that even at the best of times, she had a compelling need to feel sorry for herself.

And these were not the best of times.

In the three months since she announced her run for the White House, her campaign had come apart at the seams. While she was secretary of state, an impressive 65 percent of Americans had held a favorable view of her. Now those numbers were under water: only 42 percent were favorable and 48 percent unfavorable, and the trend line was heading in the wrong direction (by September, 59 percent of registered voters viewed Hillary unfavorably).

On top of that, Republicans in Congress demanded that Hillary testify about her culpability for the attack on the American consulate in Benghazi, which resulted in the deaths of Ambassador Christopher Stevens and three other Americans. Congress insisted she explain why she lied to the families of the dead Americans, telling them that the assault on the consulate was caused by an anti-Islamic video when she knew full well that it was planned and carried out by an al-Qaeda–affiliated terrorist group.

To make matters worse, Hillary's opponent in the Democratic primary, a seventy-four-year-old Larry David look-alike with a next-to-zero chance of winning the nomination, refused to go away. Bernie Sanders was drawing tens of thousands of people to his campaign rallies—28,000 showed up in Portland, Oregon—while the best Hillary could do was 5,500 in her adopted home state of New York.

"She's been campaigning like she was Chicken Little, with people shouting 'The sky is falling! The sky is falling!' and predicting her world is coming to an end," said one of her closest friends in an interview for this book. "Hillary's been under pressure all her life, but I've never seen her quite as shaken as this.

"She's in a rage about the FBI investigation of her emails," the friend continued. "She's worried that Obama is going to use the excuse of the FBI investigation to throw his support to someone else. She's heard that Obama has been powwowing with [Democratic senator from Massachusetts] Elizabeth Warren and [Vice President] Joe Biden.

"I've talked to Hillary about all this and she's made her position clear. 'The motherfuckers have tried to get Bill and me ever since we entered politics,' she says, 'and we've always come out smelling like roses. I'm going to beat this FBI rap, too.'"

CHAPTER

2

"An Angel Shoots a Cherub"

A Secret Service motorcade was waiting on the airport tarmac when Hillary's plane landed. Sirens blazing, a Chevrolet Suburban whisked Hillary and Huma along the shore of the Arkansas River and into the heart of Little Rock.

Huma hoped the trip would relieve Hillary of the stress brought on by her faltering campaign and the FBI investigations. After all, Little Rock was the scene of Hillary's first political victories.

Forty-two years had passed since Bill Clinton persuaded Hillary to come to Arkansas to see if she liked it well enough to move there and marry him. A recent graduate of Yale Law School, Hillary was a radical feminist who boasted that she was committed to destroying the "sexist, racist, capitalist system," and to eliminating the reign of "male supremacy." She dressed the part: when she stepped off the plane at the Little Rock airport in June 1973, she looked an absolute fright—untidy long brown hair, thick glasses, and no makeup.

By then, the twenty-five-year-old Hillary had acquired certain characteristics that would define her for the rest of her life.

She Was an Expert at Lying, Obfuscation, and Cover-Ups

Hillary pretended she came from a happy family, when in fact her father, a former Navy drill instructor, abused his wife, beat his sons, and made Hillary feel as though she was never good enough. If Hillary forgot to put the cap back on the toothpaste, her father would throw it out the window into the snow and make her go out in her bare feet and get it. Rather than reject her father's example, she embraced his pugnacious nature, even as she apparently cast conservatives and the so-called "patriarchy" in her father's abusive image.

She boasted she was named after Sir Edmund Hillary, the first man to conquer Mount Everest, when in fact she was born six years before most anyone had ever heard of Edmund Hillary, an obscure beekeeper and mountain climber in New Zealand.

And of course over the years, she changed her name nearly as often as she changed her hairstyle trying to curry favor with the public. When she was first married, she preferred to be addressed, in good feminist fashion, with her maiden name, Hillary Rodham. When that feminist stance seemed a political liability in Arkansas, she became Mrs. Bill Clinton. Later, as her own political ambitions grew, she became Hillary *Rodham* Clinton (with an emphasis on the *Rodham*). Finally, in campaign mode, she has become Hillary!—with an exclamation point, no less—one of those singular celebrities who needs but one name to identify her.

Her makeovers and fabrications—from the preposterous story about her first name to her concocted tale that she had once tried to join the Marines to her ludicrous account of how she had landed under sniper fire in Bosnia—were transparent attempts to win favor and make her appear more likeable than she was.

"I bring [Hillary's problems] down to one thing and one thing only, and that is likeability," said Peter Hart, a Democratic pollster who conducted countless focus groups on Hillary.

Or as Greg Gutfeld, the cohost of Fox News' *The Five*, put it: "[Hillary is] about as likable as elective surgery. Every time she speaks, an angel shoots a cherub."

She Was a Dyed-in-the-Wool Left-Winger

Her roommate at Wellesley College, Eleanor Acheson, the privileged granddaughter of former Secretary of State Dean Acheson, was a proud lesbian feminist who exerted an enormous influence on the development of Hillary's political ideology. (Despite persistent rumors, and the testimony of at least one of Bill Clinton's former girlfriends, no one has ever definitively proven that Hillary was or is a lesbian.)

Later, when Hillary was first lady, she persuaded Bill Clinton to appoint her old roommate Eldie Acheson to a post at the Justice Department, where she was in charge of weeding out all but the most liberal candidates for federal judgeships. In 1998, Eldie chose Emily C. Hewitt, whom she later married, to serve as a federal judge for the United States Court of Federal Claims.

While at Wellesley, Hillary became the pen pal of Saul Alinsky, the author of *Rules for Radicals*. She wrote her senior thesis on Alinsky's unscrupulous community-organizing tactics, and kept the thesis sealed from the public for the next thirty-three years. One of her former professors, and her thesis adviser, Alan Schechter, told MSNBC that suppressing the thesis "was a stupid political decision, obviously, at the time."

During a summer break at Yale, Hillary clerked at one of the country's most radical law firms, Treuhaft, Walker and Burnstein. The Oakland, California, firm had Communist Party connections and represented the Black Panthers, including an associate of Huey Newton, who was on trial for killing an Oakland police officer.

"She rejected the conservative politics of her parents when she attended Wellesley College and delivered a speech at her 1969 commencement praising herself and her classmates for rejecting 'our prevailing, acquisitive, and competitive corporate life' and 'searching for more immediate, ecstatic and penetrating modes of living,'" wrote John Podhoretz, the editor of *Commentary* magazine and a columnist for the *New York Post*. "She doesn't talk that way any longer, and she probably doesn't listen to Judy Collins (after whose version of the song 'Chelsea Morning' she and Bill named their daughter) or wear peasant dresses and clogs. But her politics and her worldview are consistent."

She Had a Disregard for the Law

After she graduated from law school, Hillary joined the staff of the Watergate committee investigating the impeachment of President Richard Nixon. She drafted a brief arguing that Nixon had no legal right to counsel during an impeachment proceeding. In order to make her case, Hillary secretly removed documents from staff files and withheld critical evidence that proved Nixon did in fact have the legal right to counsel.

Hillary's long-standing, shady relationship with the law is another lesson learned from Saul Alinsky: the law is for *other* people to follow, not for radicals. Or as Victor Davis Hanson recently noted: "Why did Mrs. Clinton, during her tenure as secretary of state, snub government protocols by using a private email account and a private server, and then permanently deleting any emails she felt were not government-related? Mrs. Clinton long ago concluded that laws in her case were to be negotiated, not obeyed."

———

The Secret Service caravan carried Hillary and Huma past the William J. Clinton Library and Presidential Center—a reminder, if Hillary needed one, that Little Rock was where she had cast aside her feminist conviction that men were inconsequential and hitched her wagon to Bill Clinton's rising star.

Little Rock was where she hired private detectives to break into the homes of women whom Bill Clinton had groped and raped in order to destroy incriminating evidence such as tape recordings and love letters from Bill.

Little Rock was where she set up a "war room," which was run by James Carville and George Stephanopoulos, to handle Bill's "bimbo eruptions." The war room smeared and blackmailed

Bill's female conquests in an effort to insulate Bill from scandal and rescue his dream of becoming president—and, not incidentally, Hillary's dream of succeeding Bill in the White House.

During Bill's first presidential run, a rock 'n' roll groupie named Connie Hamzy claimed that Bill had asked to see her breasts when he was governor of Arkansas. Stephanopoulos recalled Hillary's reaction to Hamzy's charge in his book *All Too Human*: "We have to destroy her story," Hillary said.

"Hillary Clinton's self-image as a feminist champion has always been at odds with her political partnership with a serial womanizer whose electoral career has depended on discrediting and smearing the woman with whom he's had dalliances," writes Rich Lowry, the editor of *National Review*. "Hillary was always with the sisterhood, except when one of the sisters piped up about Bill having sex with her or grossly mistreating her, in which case Hillary was with the patriarchy—i.e., her powerful, entitled husband—all the way."

Little Rock was—and always would be—Bill's stomping ground. These days when Hillary visited Little Rock (which was as infrequently as possible), she stayed at a hotel—never in the luxury penthouse on the fifth floor of the Clinton Library, because she knew that Bill used it as his love nest. She might stand by her man for political reasons, to advance her political career, because he had the charisma she lacked, but that didn't mean she needed to stay at his love shack or to have her nose rubbed in his infidelities. Their arrangement was: separate private lives, but a united political destiny.

CHAPTER

3

Her Fatal Flaw

Some literary minded observers compare Hillary to Lady Macbeth, whose vaulting ambition led to her downfall. In Hillary's case, her fatal flaw is dishonesty. She lies even when she doesn't have to.

For instance, while campaigning in Iowa, she told a group of supporters that her grandparents were immigrants to the United States.

"All of my grandparents, you know, came over here," she said. "So I sit here and I think, well you're talking about the second, third generation. That's me, that's you."

The story was untrue. One of her grandparents was an immigrant; three were not.

Another time Hillary said, "I actually started criticizing the war in Iraq before [Obama] did"—a statement that earned her a Pinocchio for lying from "The Fact Checker" in the *Washington Post*.

Hillary lied when she said that she "did not mail any classified material to anyone on my email. There is no classified material." It turned out that there were more than two thousand such documents on her email server—twenty-two of which were marked "special access program," a level of classification higher than top secret.

She lied when she said that she employed her private email "as a convenience" so that she could use a single phone for both work and personal communications. It turned out that she owned several electronic devices and that, in any case, Huma Abedin carried them for her.

She lied when she said she had *voluntarily* turned over all her work emails to the State Department. It turned out that she relinquished those emails only when forced to under subpoena, and that she withheld dozens of Benghazi-related emails she had exchanged with her back-channel fixer Sidney Blumenthal.

"Clinton has repeated numerous times that the [email] arrangement was 'allowed,' though no one in the administration has ever said they approved her server," wrote *The Hill's* A. B. Stoddard. "So Democrats—like Republicans—assume she is making a misleading statement about her own unorthodox decision to do something no Cabinet secretary had ever done before."

She lied when, according to the *New York Times*, she told the FBI that former Secretary of State Colin Powell had advised her to conduct unclassified state business using a private email account. Powell, one of the most respected elder statesmen in the country, quickly denied the report. "Her people have been trying to pin it on me," he said. "The truth is, she was using [the private email server] for a year before I sent her a memo telling her what I did."

Hillary lied when she said that as secretary of state she did not grant special favors to foreigners who donated money to the Clinton Foundation. As I documented with eyewitness accounts in *Unlikeable: The Problem with Hillary*, wealthy foreign donors who gave millions to the foundation received special treatment. One such donor was a Canadian businessman who was granted permission to sell control of 20 percent of America's uranium production capacity to Vladimir Putin's Russia. After the deal went through, Bill Clinton was invited to Moscow to give a speech. He was paid $500,000.

"The Clinton Foundation was ostensibly set up to solve the world's most pressing problems," writes David Harsanyi, senior editor at *The Federalist*. "Although it has done some fine work, it's most fruitful program has been leveraging [Hillary] Clinton's position in the State Department to enrich her family, friends and cronies. The foundation was a center of influence peddling. Rock stars. Soccer players. Conglomerates. Crown princes. All of them paid in. All of them expected access to the U.S. government."

And most of them got it.

Indeed, more than half of the private citizens who were granted access to Hillary while she was at Foggy Bottom—85 out of the 154 who got face time or spoke to her—donated to the foundation, for a total of $156 million.

The membrane that should have prevented seepage between the State Department and the foundation turned out to be totally permeable. "Laura Graham, a senior executive at the foundation," reported the *New York Post*, left almost 150 telephone messages over two years for Cheryl Mills, Hillary's chief of staff." And when Mills wasn't taking telephone calls from Graham and doing favors for foundation donors, she was traveling to New York City to interview job candidates for a top job at the foundation.

———

The impact of Hillary's menagerie of lies was reflected in public opinion polls. Sixty percent of Americans considered her "untrustworthy." And when Gallup asked Americans what word came to mind when they heard the name "Hillary Clinton," a majority replied "dishonest/liar/don't trust her/poor character."

To deal with this problem, her friends and campaign staffers set about trying to make Hillary more likeable.

"She needs to try to humanize herself, because in some ways she's kind of become a cardboard cutout figure," said liberal historian Douglas Brinkley.

But rehabilitating Hillary at this stage in her life (she turns sixty-nine on October 26) was more easily said than done.

"Hillary still obsesses about money, a narrative thread that has existed since she was thwarted in her desire to build a pool at the governor's mansion in poor Arkansas and left the White House with a doggie bag full of sofas, rugs, lamps, TVs and china, some of which the Clintons later had to pay for or return," writes *New York Times* columnist Maureen Dowd. "Even Chelsea was cashing in, getting a ridiculous, $600,000-a-year scion salary from NBC, far greater than that of many of the network's correspondents. As a Clinton White House aide once explained to me, 'Hillary, though a Methodist, thinks of herself like an Episcopal bishop who deserves to live at the level of her wealthy parishioners, in return for devoting herself to God and good works.'"

And the social critic Camille Paglia puts it this way: "So much must be overlooked or discounted—from Hillary's compulsive money-lust and her brazen indifference to normal rules to her conspiratorial use of shadowy surrogates and her sociopathic shape-shifting in policy positions for momentary expedience."

━━━

At the hotel where they stayed in Little Rock, Hillary and Huma occupied suites with an adjoining door, and early in the evening, Huma came into Hillary's bedroom.

Huma regarded herself as a fashion plate. She wore Oscar de la Renta, Catherine Malandrino, and Prada, and carried handbags by Yves Saint Laurent. Hillary, on the other hand, was notoriously neglectful of her appearance and depended on Huma to help her choose what to wear.

Some of Hillary's old acquaintances who were interviewed for this book considered Huma to be Hillary's "girlfriend." Exactly what that meant, however, depended on whom you talked to.

There were those who thought Huma and Hillary were involved in an entirely innocent relationship. "It's an older-woman-younger-woman-mother-mentor kind of thing," one of them explained.

There were others who thought that Huma and Hillary were involved in a love relationship, but one that was entirely platonic.

And then there was a small minority who concluded without any hard evidence that the relationship went beyond that.

Of course, no one except Huma and Hillary knew the exact nature of their relationship. The only evidence anyone had to go on was Huma and Hillary's behavior in public. They were constantly seen whispering in each other's ear. They giggled like schoolgirls at each other's antics. Hillary rearranged Huma's hair and frequently patted her on her lower back. They laughed about the effect these intimate gestures had on those around them.

There was no question they were joined at the hip. Huma had been by Hillary's side for the past twenty years, and she had developed an uncanny ability to anticipate—and fulfill—Hillary's needs before Hillary herself was aware of them. When Hillary lost things or forgot names or dates, which happened more frequently nowadays, Huma was always there to remedy the situation. When Hillary was unhappy with her campaign staff, Huma bitched at the offending aides.

Everyone knew that when Huma spoke, she spoke for Hillary. No one—not Bill, not Chelsea—spoke with that authority.

"Whenever I've stayed overnight in Chappaqua, I've seen just how close Huma is to Hillary," said one of Hillary's oldest friends. "Huma wakes her in the morning and curls up on the bedroom couch in a bathrobe while they go over messages and plans for the day. Huma reads Hillary their horoscopes and a selection of gushing letters that Hillary receives from young girls who admire Hillary and want to be like her.

"I'd say they are like lovers without the sex," she continued. "But the intimacy factor is intriguing. They kiss each other on the cheek. Hillary puts her arm around Huma's shoulder and whispers in her ear. I don't know what they whisper, but it's clearly something wicked, because Hillary can make Huma practically double over and laugh until it brings tears to her eyes.

"Hillary needs Huma in many ways. Her relationship with Bill is mostly business, although there are moments of tenderness. Hillary and Bill love each other, even though I'd say they are no longer *in* love.

"Both Huma and Hillary lack really honest loving relationships, and they've found each other and they lavish each other with love. Hillary's never been a big fan of sex. She told me when we were at school together that she found it messy and embarrassing. But she does love affection and she gets it from Huma."

With her exotic beauty and expensive, high fashion wardrobe, Huma intrigued members of the Washington press corps. They wrote stories about her, but they did not explore the intimate nature of her relationship with Hillary. There was an unspoken pact that it was off limits. In an era in which social media left nothing to the imagination, this starchy attitude toward the Hillary-Huma connection was a throwback to the days when reporters did not write about the intimate lives of politicians like John F. Kennedy.

But that didn't stop people from gossiping everywhere in Washington, including in the Residence of the Obama White House.

"Valerie [Jarrett] says it's absolutely embarrassing how much Hillary fawns over Huma and insists that she be in on any meeting, even at the White House," said a source who spoke to Jarrett on a regular basis and dined with her in Washington. "Huma has to be there or very nearby. And Huma acts like a puppy dog. Valerie and Michelle laugh about how *Game of Thrones* the relationship is—Huma is such a courtesan. Valerie says—and I'm quoting—'It's uncomfortable being around those two.'"

▰▰▰

For Hillary' s appearance tonight, Huma picked out a loose-fitting royal blue tunic with a mandarin collar and a pair of diamond earrings.

Accompanied by a phalanx of Secret Service agents, Hillary and Huma climbed into a Chevrolet Suburban and, with the lights of the motorcade flashing in the dusk, headed across the Arkansas River toward the twin city of North Little Rock.

Clusters of Arkansans lined the sidewalks and waved as the motorcade roared by. But unlike Bill Clinton, who often got out of his car to press the flesh when he was in Little Rock, Hillary ignored the crowds and didn't bother to wave back.

Inside the vast Verizon Arena, a painting of Hillary done by a local artist named Sean Shrum had just been auctioned off for

$19,000, and the swarm of alcohol-fueled Democrats roared their approval when they spotted Hillary making her entrance.

As she reached the stage, the expression on her face changed from a fixed grimace to a frozen smile. The man who introduced her, former Arkansas Governor Mike Beebe, reminded Hillary that she was among friends. There wasn't a single right-wing conspirator in the crowd. Everyone in the 18,000-seat arena had happily paid to hear her talk.

It was the perfect opportunity for Hillary to speak from the heart.

"When Chelsea was a baby," Hillary began, reading from a teleprompter, "I sang to her every night. I sat in a rocking chair, singing my heart out to her before I put her to bed...."

And she felt no guilt or shame about making up the entire story. Hillary never sang lullabies to Chelsea. She left that up to Bill. In his Clinton biography, *First in His Class*, David Maraniss quotes a family friend who overheard Bill singing a lullaby to his infant daughter: "I want a div-or-ce, I want a div-or-or-or-ce."

PART 2

BILL

*It's often said, by people trying to show how grown-up
and unshocked they are, that all Clinton did to get himself
impeached was lie about sex. That's not really true. What he
actually lied about, in the perjury that also got him disbarred,
was the women. And what this involved was a steady campaign
of defamation, backed up by private dicks (you should excuse
the expression) and salaried government employees, against
women who I believe were telling the truth.*

—"The Case Against Hillary Clinton," Christopher Hitchens

CHAPTER
4

Kale Salad and a Massage

ill Clinton was getting a foot massage.

"We were on the terrace of his apartment," recalled the twenty-something intern at the William J. Clinton Presidential Library and Museum who was massaging Bill's feet. "We had a meal served from 42 [the restaurant in the Little Rock library]—vegan stuff like kale salad.

"He often invites girls like me who work at the library to his apartment for a glass of red wine and a massage," the intern said in an interview for this book. "He likes his neck and shoulders massaged because he gets knots in his muscles. But what he really likes is to have his feet massaged. He just kicks off his loafers and socks and puts his feet on the coffee table. That really makes him happy.

· "Bill is always flirting with the women at the library. He knows everybody by their first name and is incredibly kind and generous. When he talks to you, it's like you are the only person in the world. I always called him Mr. President, naturally, but one day he looked at me with this horny look and said, 'Call me Bill.' I sort of knew then that I was in.

"I know what people would say if they knew I gave him a foot massage. But, hey, if it makes him happy, I'm happy to do it. The idea of touching the president of the United States that way is incredibly exciting to me."

In the midst of the massage, the phone rang. Clinton listened for a moment, then put down the receiver.

"Damn!" he said, according to the intern's recollection.

"What's wrong?" she asked.

"Hillary just told a bunch of Iowa Democrats she's on Snapchat," Clinton said.

"So what?" the young intern said. "I'm on Snapchat. *Everybody's* on Snapchat."

"Yeah, but she said she loves Snapchat because all her emails disappear by themselves," Clinton said.

"I still don't understand," the intern said.

"Just keep doing what you're doing," Clinton said.

While the intern went back to massaging his feet, Clinton made another call. He informed the person on the other end of the line that Hillary had cracked a joke about her disappearing emails at the Wing Ding dinner in Clear Lake, Iowa.

The intern remembered Clinton saying: "She's fucking over the FBI. How stupid is that! You and I need to talk. I'll send a plane to get you."

CHAPTER
5

Blindsided

The man who arrived at the library was one of Bill Clinton's oldest and most trusted advisers.* They strolled out onto Clinton's penthouse terrace, his friend carrying a tumbler of Johnny Walker Black, Bill with a glass of red wine, which his doctor had prescribed for his heart.

"You're right, this email thing is spiraling out of control," the adviser said, according to his recollection of the meeting, which he later shared with the author of this book.

"From what I know of the case," he went on, "she's extremely vulnerable. It involves not only the FBI and the Justice Department, but two inspectors general in the intelligence community

---

* The source was interviewed more than two dozen times for this book.

and the inspector general of the State Department. There are a number of statutes that she appears to have violated and national security laws that she may have breached."

He took out several sheets of paper and began reading from a long list that amounted to a bill of indictment:

- Flouting federal laws governing record-keeping requirements.
- Failing to preserve emails sent or received from her personal accounts, as required by law.
- Circumventing the Freedom of Information Act.
- Instructing her aides to send classified materials on her unsecure network.
- Running afoul of the "gross negligence" clause of the Espionage Act (which meant prosecutors would not have to prove "intent" to find her guilty).
- Pretending she didn't know that Sensitive Compartmented Information (SCI) was classified.
- Transferring classified material that originated at the CIA, the National Security Agency, and other intelligence sources, to her unsecured network.
- Authoring hundreds of emails with classified information to people who did not have security clearance.
- Lying to the FBI.
- Inducing aides to commit perjury.
- Engaging in public corruption by using the office of secretary of state to feather the nest of the Clinton family foundation.

When his friend had finished ticking off the items on his list, Clinton asked: "So?"

"My recommendation is that Hillary get ahead of the situation by hiring an outside legal counsel," the adviser replied, recalling the conversation for the author of this book. "She needs to secure the services of an expert legal counsel—preferably a big-league defense attorney from the Republican side of the aisle."

Hillary, he added, *needed to get some "discovery" as to where the investigation was going.*

"You don't want to be blindsided, and if you ignore it, pretend it's a partisan ploy, and act scornfully it *will* blindside you," the adviser said. "That's not where you want to be."

Clinton said he worried that Hillary depended for legal advice on their old Yale Law School classmate, David Kendall, who had advised Bill Clinton during the Lewinsky scandal and represented him during his impeachment trial. There were major problems with Kendall. First, Kendall had kept a thumb drive with Hillary's classified emails in an unsecure safe at his law firm. That exposed him to a possible criminal indictment by the Department of Justice. And second, Kendall didn't like soiling his hands dealing with the media. That was a big drawback, because as far as Bill Clinton was concerned, Hillary's problems were as much about the *appearance* of the facts as they were about the *actual* facts.

"Hillary has been treating this FBI investigation like it's some kind of hit job by right-wing nuts," Clinton said, according to his friend's recollection. "Her take on the problem comes from the advice of her political operatives, not me. They keep telling her she's above it all, and that there's no way she's vulnerable."

By joking about it and pretending it's some made-up political spin, Clinton said, *Hillary's only hurting herself with the prosecutors.*

"Insulting career FBI and Justice Department investigators is a bad strategy," he said. "[General David] Petraeus's situation comes to mind. He lied to the FBI, got slammed with a misdemeanor and a big fine, and saw his career go down the toilet. And *his* violations of national security were probably far less complex and intolerable than Hillary's."

∎

"Hillary's emails aside, there was a big problem with her campaign," his adviser told the author of this book. "Bill knew—even if Hillary didn't—that he had to be a major component of her campaign for it to work. He felt that the country had drifted to extremes on both sides and the only winning strategy was to persuade voters on the basis of their hearts—to be so appealing and likeable they wanted to see you on television in their living rooms every night. He believed that *he* had that appeal. But he was far from certain that he had the stamina to do as much campaigning as needed to be done.

"The other component was the growing distance between Bill and Hillary," the adviser continued. "She didn't listen to much of what he said anymore. When he went on about policy and politics, she rolled her eyes and started checking messages on her BlackBerry.

"She resented the fact that Bill was treated like a rock star and that she had to work hard to create the illusion of enthusiasm. All Bill had to do is walk into a room. He gave off an electrical charge. Men lit up in his presence. Women swooned. Hillary had to scream to get attention.

"I think that if Hillary was more appreciative of Bill's efforts and less resentful, he would've worked harder for her. It was exhausting to work for someone who didn't appreciate you.

"I was with him at the apartment in Little Rock after a long telephone conversation with Hillary in which he held the phone away from his ear because she was shouting that he was interfering with her campaign. Finally, he cut her short and said he would call back later. He didn't exactly hang up on her, but it was very close.

"Afterward, he slumped down in a chair and shook his head. He looked old and defeated. Then he got up, went out to his rooftop putting green, and started chipping shots into the Arkansas River. When he was done, he looked like his old self again.

"He said, 'She can do whatever the fuck she wants,' and he started talking about his plans for building a swimming pool on the roof of the library. He wants to have naked pool parties the way JFK had pool parties when he was in the White House.

"He had an architect give him a feasibility report on building a pool, and it turned out that it would have been very expensive to build and disruptive to the functioning of the library. Anyway, the National Archives, which administers presidential libraries, probably would have vetoed the idea. So he dropped the plan. But for a while, he thought about getting an above-ground pool for the girls to splash around in.

"Bill has a bunch of women he regularly invites to his apartment. Most of them are young and good looking. He loves being surrounded by pretty girls. The place is completely secure so he knows there's no chance any photographers can get in.

"I was there at one of his parties on a hot steamy day. He served champagne and cold beer and handed out roses, which he grows on the terrace and which are named after his mother Virginia Kelly.

At one point he got out a hose and sprayed some of the girls.

"'Keep that up,' I told him, 'and you're going to have the first wet T-shirt contest ever held at a presidential library.'"

CHAPTER
6

Broken Promises

ill Clinton arrived in Martha's Vineyard in a cheerful mood.

He was looking forward to celebrating the eightieth birthday of Vernon Jordan, the civil rights activist, Washington insider, and one of Bill's favorite people. The plan was for Bill to join a golf foursome that included Jordan, former U.S. Trade Representative Ron Kirk, and one of Bill's *least* favorite people, Barack Obama.

There was bad blood between the Clintons and the Obamas. Several Washington journalists, who were eager to stay on the good side of the Clintons in the event they made it back to the White House, had tipped off Bill that Valerie Jarrett was the original source of many of the damaging stories about Hillary's use of a private email account and her pay-to-play shenanigans with the Clinton Foundation while she was secretary of state. And Jarrett didn't stop there. As I reported in *Unlikeable: The Problem with Hillary*, when Monica Lewinsky suddenly resurfaced after years of living in obscurity, Jarrett put out word through intermediaries that the White House would look with favor if the media gave Monica some ink and airtime. The media quickly obliged: *Vanity Fair* invited Monica to attend its annual Oscar party and write an essay titled "Shame and Survival," and the National Geographic Channel featured Monica in a special called "The 90's: The Last Great Decade?"

News that the anti-Hillary leaks originated in the White House didn't surprise Bill. It only confirmed his view that Obama would go to any lengths to dislodge Hillary as the Democratic Party's nominee.

The Clintons and the Obamas had a history of broken promises and festering resentments. Bill had delivered a rousing speech for Obama at the 2012 Democratic Party convention in return for Obama's promise to endorse Hillary in 2016, something Obama had not yet done, and would not do until after Bernie Sanders had gone down to defeat in the Democratic primaries and there was no alternative. Bill never forgave him.

As for Obama, he had paid off Hillary's 2008 campaign debt and made her his secretary of state, but as far as he was concerned, he had gotten little or nothing in return. Bill and Hillary acted as though Obama's presidency was a mere interregnum between Clinton I and Clinton II.

Most important of all, the Clintons and the Obamas were engaged in a power struggle over control of the Democratic Party. The stakes were enormous: thousands of elected offices and official positions, hundreds of thousands of patronage jobs, and millions of dollars in commissions, consultancies, and advisory fees. Not to mention the power to decide the future direction of the party.

If Hillary won the White House, Obama said, according to a source close to Jarrett, *the Clintons would make sure that he'd be marginalized in his own party. He couldn't let that happen. He had to find someone to replace Hillary as the party's nominee.*

"This election is the last roundup for the Clintons," Obama said. "Take away their hope of future power, and their family foundation and speaking fees will dry up. They'll be a thing of the past. But I'll still be the head of the party."

When they couldn't avoid being seen together in public, Bill Clinton and Barack Obama acted as though all was sweetness and light.

"I'll just bite my lip and act like everything is fine," Bill said to a friend, who accompanied him on the flight to Martha's Vineyard.

As his plane landed, Bill's cell phone rang. He answered it, and his face instantly turned bright red.

"The *fucker!*" he said.

"What happened?" he was asked.

"The word in Washington is that Obama's preparing to say that Biden would make a fine president," Clinton said.

Bill immediately put in a call to Hillary, who was campaigning in Iowa, to tell her the news. He listened for a moment and then, with a big smile, put away the phone.

"You're not going to believe this," he said, chuckling. "Hillary just threw a flower vase across her hotel room."

■■■

A small but enthusiastic group of people was gathered at the Farm Neck Country Club when Bill's motorcade drew up to the entrance. He worked the crowd, shaking hands and signing autographs.

Inside, he spotted Vernon Jordan who, at 6-foot-4, was hard to miss. Jordan was a unique figure in American politics—the first black man to be accepted as a full-fledged member of the Washington establishment. Jordan and Clinton had a lot in common. They shared a love of politics, dirty jokes, and the company of beautiful women.

On the golf course, Bill gave Obama a perfunctory greeting, and Obama responded in kind. After they had teed off, Bill turned to Obama and asked if it was true that he planned to endorse Joe Biden or Elizabeth Warren for president. According to a source who spoke to Bill afterward, Obama replied, "I'm not endorsing. I told Hillary that."

As Bill later reconstructed the conversation, the two presidents exchanged the following heated words:

Clinton: Where is this email crap going legally?

Obama: I really don't know. [Laughing dismissively] I have other things to worry about.

Clinton: You brought this on us, Hillary and me. No investigation gets started without your approval. I was president and I know how the goddamn thing works. Don't think for a minute I don't.

"I was so angry that I was swinging my arms around, and I could see the Secret Service guys were getting antsy," Bill later recalled in a conversation with a source who was interviewed for this book. "My heart was beating so loud I could hear it. But I was really angry with myself, because I had just given Hillary hell for making the FBI investigation worse, and here I had insulted the president, who was going to be Hillary's judge and jury on the emails. I'd fallen into the same trap. I was sick about it."

PART 3

BARACK

Obama has always resented the idea that it mattered for him to charm and knead and whip and hug and horse-trade his way to legislative victories, to lubricate the levers of government with personal loyalty. But, once more, he learned the hard way, it matters.

—Maureen Dowd

CHAPTER
7

"Love Joe Biden"

It was Stephen Colbert's first week as the host of *The Late Show*, and his producers were looking for a big "get"—the kind of guest who could reel in humongous ratings. They called around to the usual suspects, movie stars and musical artists, and they even tried the White House. Obama wasn't available.

But how about Joe Biden?

The producers at CBS jumped at the chance to get Joe. Ever since his forty-six-year-old son Beau succumbed to brain cancer in May, there had been a torrent of sympathy for the vice president. Millions of viewers were sure to tune in to hear the story of how Joe balanced the inexpressible heartbreak of losing a son against the siren call of the presidency.

Could Joe Biden climb out of his dark abyss in time to challenge Hillary Clinton?

Now *that* was reality television.

"How did you maintain your real soul in a city so filled with people who are trying to lie to us in subtle ways?" a fawning Stephen Colbert asked Biden.

"What always confuses me about folks I've worked with is why in God's name would you want the job if you couldn't say what you believed?" Biden said in a not-so-subtle dig at Hillary Clinton, whose inauthenticity and expanding email scandal were reflected in her sinking poll numbers. "I'm not—there's nothing noble about this, but ask yourselves this question: Would you want a job that, in fact, every day you had to get up and to modulate what you said and believed?"

———

Stephen Colbert wasn't the only one who was keen to see Joe Biden run for president. According to columnist Maureen Dowd, Beau Biden's dying wish was that his father run and save the country from the Clintons. As Dowd wrote:

> When Beau realized he was not going to make it, he asked his father if he had a minute to sit down and talk.
>
> "Of course, honey," the vice president replied.
>
> At the table, Beau told his dad he was worried about him.

My kid's dying, an anguished Joe Biden thought to himself, *and he's making sure I'm O.K.*

"Dad, I know you don't give a damn about money," Beau told him, dismissing the idea that his father would take some sort of cushy job after the vice presidency to cash in.

Beau was losing his nouns and the right side of his face was partially paralyzed. But he had a mission: He tried to make his father promise to run, arguing that the White House should not revert to the Clintons and that the country would be better off with Biden values.

There was no mystery about how Dowd obtained that fly-on-the-wall account of Beau's deathbed conversation with his dad. It could only have come from one person, Joe Biden, who had told the story—*in private*—on several previous occasions.

Biden was eager to honor Beau's wishes, but he admitted to a close family friend (who was also a friend of the author of this book)* that he wasn't sure he had it in him to run for president. Even if he could pull himself together and move beyond his grief and anger over Beau's loss, did he really want to risk his reputation?

"Right now," he said, according to his friend, "I'm more popular than I've ever been. Do I want to leave office with my reputation intact, or do I want to get down in the mud with Hillary? Because if I run, you can be sure all the old shit comes back."

---

* The source was interviewed five times on the subject of Biden's ambivalence about running for president.

He was right. Hillary had already given David Brock, her pasty-faced Reich minister of propaganda, permission to attack Joe. And Brock wasted no time disgorging his oppo research.

Back in 1988, Biden had been forced to drop out of the race for the Democratic nomination after it was revealed he had lifted five pages from a published article for a term paper at law school, and had plagiarized speeches by British Labor leader Neil Kinnock, Robert Kennedy, and Hubert Humphrey.

According to Brock, African Americans and other minorities wouldn't vote for Biden once they were reminded that as a senator he had favored mandatory minimum sentences for federal crimes, which resulted in high incarceration rates for blacks.

Feminists would be outraged when they were reminded of Biden's shabby treatment of Anita Hill, who had accused U.S. Supreme Court nominee Clarence Thomas of sexual harassment.

Supporters of President Obama would be shocked when they were reminded that Biden had been reluctant to support the raid that killed Osama bin Laden.

True to form, Brock—aided by Sidney ("Sid Vicious") Blumenthal and other denizens of what Maureen Dowd called the Clinton "Slime Room"—began throwing dirt on Biden practically before the dirt had settled on Beau Biden's casket.

███

To test the political waters, Biden invited Elizabeth Warren, the firebrand senator from Massachusetts, for lunch at his official residence on the grounds of the United States Naval Observatory.

They discussed where they stood on issues like the economy and foreign affairs, and Biden put out a feeler about choosing Warren as his running mate if he ran. For whatever reason—probably because he was so unsure of his own mind—he did not make Warren an outright offer.

Since Warren became a United States senator in 2013, she had assumed Ted Kennedy's mantle as the conscience of the progressive wing of the Democratic Party. She had enormous power in shaping legislation and deciding the fate of White House nominations.

She was underwhelmed by Biden's half-hearted offer. Being his vice president, she thought, would amount to a step down from her current position of power; she would be a Biden functionary rather than the progressives' heroine of the Senate.

▬▬▬▬

By the end of the summer of 2015, Joe still hadn't made up his mind. Among his close advisers, Steve Ricchetti, his chief of staff, told him that he still had time to enter the presidential contest. It wouldn't be easy, but he had a shot at beating Hillary for the nomination.

The Iowa caucuses were five months away, Hillary was proving to be the the weakest Democrat candidate in three decades—since Walter Mondale ran in 1984—and the party's primary campaign was in a state of flux. Behind the scenes, the Clintons and the Obamas had yet to call a truce to their long-running blood feud, and Obama was actively searching for an attractive candidate who could crush Hillary at the polls.

Obama had several candidates in mind: Brian Schweitzer, the progressive senator from Montana; Deval Patrick, the former governor of Massachusetts and a personal friend of Obama's; Elizabeth Warren; and Joe Biden.

As the constant drip, drip, drip of Hillary's email scandal ate away at her popular appeal, Biden emerged as Obama's first choice. More than the others on Obama's wish list, Joe had the chops (thirty-five years as a senator, seven years as vice president), the poll numbers (a 60 percent favorability rating), and a lifelong craving to be president. What's more, Joe had proved himself to be a most loyal lieutenant. If elected, he'd represent a third Obama term.

During a White House briefing, Press Secretary Josh Earnest made a startling pronouncement.

"The president has indicated that his view that the decision that he made, I guess seven years ago now, to add Joe Biden to the ticket as his running mate was the smartest decision that he has ever made in politics," Earnest said. "And I think that should give you some sense into the president's view into the vice president's aptitude for the top job."

In case some members of the White House press corps missed the point, Earnest drove it home. "There is no one in American politics today," he said, "who has a better understanding of exactly what is required to mount a successful national presidential campaign" than Joe Biden.

Both publicly and privately, Obama did everything in his power to nudge the grief-stricken Biden in the direction of running. Valerie Jarrett recommended a psychiatrist to help Biden deal with his crushing depression. And Obama offered to help the vice president pay off the mountain of medical bills he had incurred during the long months of Beau's battle with brain cancer.

As Biden told the story, he and his wife Jill were thinking of selling their Delaware home to pay the medical bills. "[Obama] got up and said, 'Don't sell that house,'" Biden recalled, according to the *New York Post.* "'Promise me you won't sell the house. I'll give you the money. Whatever you need. I'll give you the money. Don't, Joe—promise me. . . .' I said, 'I don't think we're going to have to anyway.' He said, 'Promise me.'"

"President Barack Obama says he has no preference in the Democratic fight to succeed him," wrote Alex Wayne in Bloomberg Politics. "Hillary Clinton could be forgiven for having her doubts.

"Since the start of September, the White House has dispatched Biden on photo-op trips to Democratic bastions in Florida, Pennsylvania, New York, and this week, California, Michigan, and Ohio," Wayne continued. "Last week, Biden met in New York with Robert Wolf, a top Wall Street fundraiser for Obama. And last Wednesday, when Obama took Biden's wife, Jill, on a trip to Michigan to promote the idea of free community college, he reminded the audience of his feelings toward his vice president.

"'Her husband is not so bad, either. He's OK,' Obama deadpanned. 'Love Joe Biden.'"

■

When Stephen Colbert returned from a commercial break, he reintroduced Biden, and the audience in the Ed Sullivan Theater in New York City broke into a chant: *"Joe! Joe! Joe! Joe!"*

Biden laughed and said, "Be careful what you wish for."

"Being close to the president," Colbert said, "that's one job that preps you for…Do you have anything you'd like to tell us about your plans?"

"Yes, I think *you* should run for president," replied Biden, poking fun at Colbert, who ran a satirical presidential race in 2008 on the Comedy Central network. "And I'll be your vice president," Biden added.

But Colbert wouldn't let Biden off the hook so easily.

What about the presidency? asked Colbert. Was Biden emotionally ready to take the plunge?

"Look, I don't think any man or woman should run for president," said Biden, "unless, number one, they know exactly why they would want to be president and two, they can look at folks out there and say, 'I promise you have my whole heart, my whole soul, my energy, and my passion.' And I'd be lying if I said that I knew I was there."

███████

He wasn't there yet.

There were endless discussions among Biden, Obama, and Jarrett about whether it was possible for Joe to make up for Hillary's advantages in fundraising, data mining, and her ground game. Finally, after weeks of Biden's Hamlet-like behavior, Jarrett lost her patience and told him, in effect, to snap out of it.

"If the president winks and nods, you can make up for everything—lost time, lost money, lost organization," she told Biden, according to his recollection of their meeting.

Biden nodded, but remained unconvinced.

The president could wink and nod all he wanted to, he told Jarrett, but the only way Obama could absolutely assure Biden that he would win the nomination was if Obama could absolutely promise that Hillary was going to be indicted.

———

At about this time, Hillary requested a meeting with Obama.

"Barack threw a major fit in the Oval," said a source who spoke frequently with Jarrett. "He couldn't believe the audacity Hillary had even to ask. She obviously wanted to talk about the FBI investigation, and to ask him to intervene on her behalf.

"Barack almost never loses it," the source continued. "But this time he did. He got up from his desk and threw a rubber ball that he often plays with across the room.

"'Goddamn the Clintons!' he yelled. 'Tell them to go to hell! She's lied about everything.'

"He continued pacing the floor of the Oval. Then he turned to Valerie and said, 'Make sure that any smidgen of wrongdoing that's in Hillary's files is turned over to the Justice Department and the FBI. *Everything.*'"

Jarrett did as she was told, and word came back from Attorney General Loretta Lynch that Obama shouldn't get his hopes up too high. The FBI was six months into its investigation, and from what Lynch could ascertain, Jim Comey still hadn't decided whether to recommend indictments against Hillary.

What were the odds against Hillary? Jarrett asked Lynch.

About fifty-fifty, said the attorney general.

Jarrett told Obama who told Biden.

Fifty-fifty wasn't good enough for Biden.

And on October 21, with a stiff and expressionless Barack Obama standing by his side in the Rose Garden, Biden took himself out of the race.

CHAPTER

8

The Smell Test

"It felt like a crisis meeting—grim, serious, no small talk or jokes."

The speaker was Elizabeth Warren, and she was describing a meeting with President Obama and Valerie Jarrett in the Oval Office. As Warren recalled the encounter, which she described to friends, the man David Axelrod had dubbed No Drama Obama was in an irascible mood.

"I'm fed up with the Hillary soap opera," Warren recalled Obama saying.

Hillary had done something that went beyond selfish and stupid, he told Warren. She had endangered the safety of her country by using an unsecure email system that could be hacked by the Russians, the Chinese, the Iranians, and God knew who else.

But he couldn't appear to interfere with the FBI's investigation; that would open him to charges of obstructing justice. What he could do was encourage the State Department and the intelligence community to give their full cooperation to the FBI.

"Still," Obama said, "an indictment is a maybe. But you Elizabeth—*you* can beat her."

Many in the Democratic Party believed that Elizabeth Warren could take Hillary down if she got into the race.

Where Hillary was wooden and uninspiring, Warren was a spellbinding orator.

Where Hillary mouthed progressive platitudes, Warren actually believed in them.

Where Hillary rehashed Bernie Sanders's tirade about income inequality, Warren was the one who had coined the phrase "the rigged economy."

Where Hillary was a throwback to the left-of-center Clintonite Democratic Party, Warren was the personification of a party that had lurched so far to the left that Debbie Wasserman Schultz, then the chairwoman of the Democratic National Committee, couldn't tell Chris Matthews of MSNBC the difference between a Democrat and a socialist.

The party had been taken over by militant left-wing groups like Occupy Wall Street, Black Lives Matter, the Service Employees

International Union, the Sierra Club, and Emily's List. And those groups adored Elizabeth Warren. Whenever she spoke, they bellowed: *"Run, Liz, run! Run, Liz, Run!"*

It was heady stuff for a former academic whose greatest ambition in life had once been to head the Consumer Financial Protection Bureau. Now, Hollywood moguls and movie stars offered to give her fundraising parties, and billionaires like George Soros, who was voted "the single most destructive leftist demagogue in the country" by readers of *Human Events*, were at her beck and call.

And yet, Warren hesitated to throw her hat in the ring.

Her hesitation had nothing to do with a concern about getting on the wrong side of the Clintons. She wasn't particularly fond of Hillary. Back in the late 1990s, when Hillary was first lady, she promised Warren to block legislation that favored the credit-card industry and its confiscatory interest rates. Hillary convinced President Clinton to veto the legislation. But as soon as Hillary became a senator from New York and depended on contributions from banking industry executives, she did a flip-flop and came out in favor of the bill.

Warren never trusted Hillary after that.

■■■■

The truth was, Elizabeth Warren hesitated to run because she couldn't pass the smell test.

Few people were aware of her past record. For example, the Elizabeth Warren who captured the hearts of progressives with her fiery anti-capitalist rhetoric and condemnation of Wall Street speculators was the same Elizabeth Warren who had made a fortune buying foreclosed homes and flipping them for a profit.

"Warren…has built a political career on denouncing the sort of banking titans and financial sophisticates who make a buck off the little guy," wrote Jillian Kay Melchior and Eliana Johnson in *National Review*. "[But] Warren bought and sold at least five properties for profit at a different time in her life, before the cratering economy and a political career made her a star."

The *Boston Herald* ran stories about Warren's house-flipping exploits during her campaign for the United States Senate in 2012. The paper noted that Warren invested in "the often topsy-turvy real-estate market of the 1990s" and that her actions "don't seem to square with her public statements about the latest real estate boom and bust."

Or take another example: the Elizabeth Warren who railed against the deceit and deception of bankers was the same Elizabeth Warren who lied that she was the great-great-great granddaughter of a Cherokee Indian, making her 1/32 Native American. No such great-great-great Indian grandmother existed. But Warren used her claim to membership in a racial minority to bag an affirmative-action post as a teacher at Harvard.

"Fauxcahontas put up a new TV ad this week," wrote Boston columnist and radio host Howie Carr. "In it, Liz Warren shares the pain her supposed Indian heritage has caused—why her parents had to elope because her dad's family didn't want their son marrying a girl with Indian blood. Huh. Twila Barnes, an indefatigable Cherokee genealogist, dug up the 1932 wedding notice in the Oklahoma papers. Warren's folks got hitched in a large Protestant church."

Or take yet another example: the Elizabeth Warren who decried the excesses of Wall Street was the same Elizabeth Warren who was a millionaire and lived with her second husband, Bruce Mann, a law professor, in a $2.4-million home in one of the poshest neighborhoods of Cambridge, Massachusetts.

She employed two housekeepers, a cook, and a gardener, and her treatment of her help said a lot about her attitude toward the put-upon of the world whom she claimed to champion.

"She may say she's for the little people, but she doesn't treat her help very well, I can tell you that," said a housekeeper who worked for Warren until recently and was interviewed for this book. "No matter how hard you work, it's never good enough. The bed isn't made right, the sheets are too loose. She acts like it's a military thing. When she gets mad, she screams and yells and calls a maid or cook an idiot.

"One of the worst things she does is misplace a blouse or a sweater and then accuse the household help of putting it someplace where she can't find it," the housekeeper continued. "It's almost like being accused of stealing.

"Most of the time, she seems a bit out of it. She has Post-it notes all over the house to remind her of things she has to do or wants done for her. There are notes on the refrigerator reminding her to ask the cook to make a pot roast, notes on the bathroom door reminding her to order towels. On her office door, there are notes with names and phone numbers for people to call. Sometimes she walks around the house writing notes and sticking them up.

"Believe me, the turnover in her household staff is pretty amazing. Gardeners, maids, cooks all come and go."

Obama was aware of Warren's political baggage. But now that Joe Biden was unavailable, Warren was his last great hope.

Was she endorsing Hillary? Obama asked her.

No.

Was she staying neutral?

Yes.

Was she thinking of running for president herself?

No.

Why not?

Just don't think it's my time.

"Elizabeth, I see the fire and the energy in you for a successful run," Obama said, according to Warren's recollection. "The base [of the party] loves you."

"That may be true," Warren remembered replying. "But God help me if I wind up running."

Later, Warren confided to close friends—among them, several members of the Kennedy family, who were interviewed for this book—that Obama promised her the sun and the moon if she would challenge Hillary for the nomination.

"I said thanks but no thanks," Warren told the Kennedys. "And it wasn't even close."

CHAPTER

9

A One-Eighty

"**A**fter Joe and Elizabeth turned him down, Barack lived in a state of complete denial," Valerie Jarrett confided to a close friend.* "He dreamed about some fresh face coming out of nowhere, some young and charismatic politician, preferably black, but not necessarily black, someone like him, the way he did back in 2007. But the cavalry never arrived."

Obama briefly toyed with the idea of supporting Bernie Sanders, either covertly or overtly, in his primary contest against Hillary. Maybe Bernie could motivate Obama's old coalition and persuade its members to fall in love with him. But Jarrett's pollsters

---

* Jarrett's friend regularly spoke to her on the phone, dined with her when he was in Washington, and was occasionally invited to sleep in the Lincoln bedroom.

assured her that that wasn't possible. The black vote wasn't going to come out for Bernie. And the idea of Middle America voting for a socialist was a fantasy.

But politics was like the weather—unpredictable—and Obama played in his mind with various scenarios. What if, against the odds, Bernie somehow snatched the nomination away from Hillary at the Democratic National Convention? Or what if Hillary was indicted and the party establishment replaced her as the nominee? Or if Joe Biden changed his mind and parachuted into the convention to accept the nomination and Bernie's army of supporters bolted and formed a third party?

If any of those "what ifs" happened, the Democrats would almost certainly suffer a crushing defeat at the polls.

And yet, Obama couldn't bring himself to put aside his feud with the Clintons, accept the inevitable, and endorse Hillary. He wasn't ready to forgive and forget. As I wrote in *Blood Feud: The Clintons vs. the Obamas*:

> This was a family fight, and as the saying goes, no one fights dirtier or more brutally than blood. Like all family squabbles, this one was about power, money, and primacy. Obama's legacy hung in the balance. If the Clintons captured control of the Democratic Party and returned to the White House, they would try to expunge much of Obama's legacy; they would try to make him a historic anomaly—America's first black president—in a sixteen-year interregnum between the two Clinton regimes.

To someone as vain and self-admiring as Obama, conceding victory to the Clintons would amount to more than a humiliating defeat. It would be political suicide. It was an idea he could not bear.

———

Late at night in the Family Residence, after Obama had excused himself and gone to bed, Valerie Jarrett and Michelle Obama opened a bottle of Chardonnay and discussed Obama's turmoil and the toll it was taking on his mind and body.

He was having trouble sleeping. Michelle insisted that he ask his doctor for sleeping pills, which he did. He was prescribed Ambien. He told Michelle that he took the pills, but she didn't believe him. He was taking Melatonin, which did no good. So, he was tossing and turning in his sleep, and she had to get up and go to the Queen's Bedroom to sleep.

Michelle was concerned that the president wasn't getting enough sleep, and that he was struggling at times to stay awake during meetings about subjects that didn't interest him.

She told Jarrett that she was counting the days until their term in the White House was over. Until then, however, Michelle and Valerie agreed, Barack had to face reality.

He had to take three major actions.

First, he had to swallow his pride and endorse Hillary as the party's nominee.

Second, he had to rally his coalition of young people, college graduates, African Americans, Hispanics, and other minorities, and persuade them to come out and vote for Hillary.

And third, he had to reverse his position on the FBI investigation of Hillary's emails, and make Attorney General Loretta Lynch understand that no matter what evidence the FBI turned up, Hillary had to get off without suffering any legal punishment or injury.

"It was up to us—Michelle and I—to persuade him," Jarrett said, according to the description of her conversation with Michelle that she conveyed to her close friend. "He always listened to us, but we knew that this time it was going to be a hard sell. I hate telling Barack what he doesn't want to hear. I knew this was going to be the most painful talk I'd ever had with him."

▬▬▬

The next night, they had the talk.

"I felt as though I was forcing Barack to eat a toad," Jarrett recalled, "but I told him he had no alternative: if he wanted a Democrat to follow him in the White House, he had to endorse Hillary.

"There was a lot of shouting and pacing of the floor and banging of the desk, but after he calmed down, I told him there was something else he had to do," Jarrett said. "He had to authorize me to tell Lynch that we were doing a one-eighty on Hillary. No indictment, no matter what."

What if Comey threatened to resign?

In that event, Jarrett said, Obama could give Hillary a pardon.

"A presidential pardon would put an end to the legal process," Jarrett said.

"That'll be great for Hillary," Obama said, "but what about me? I'll be declaring war on the FBI."

PART 4

"BIG JIM"

We're conducting an investigation. That's the bureau's business. That's what we do. It's in our name.

—FBI Director James Comey responding to Hillary Clinton's claim that the FBI's probe of her private email server was a mere "security inquiry"

CHAPTER
10

Collision Course

It was six o'clock at night and Elizabeth Shapiro, one of the Justice Department's prosecutors handling the Hillary Clinton email investigation, was getting ready to pack up and go home when her phone rang.

The caller was an assistant to James Comey.

"The director wants to see you in his office," the assistant said.

"*Now?*" Shapiro asked.

"Yes, *now!*"

"I groaned," Shapiro later recalled to a colleague, who spoke to the author of this book. "Jim has a way of summoning people to his office late in the afternoon, and no one ever says no to Jim. I called home and said it was going to be a late night."

As Betsy (as everyone called her) left her office at Justice on this chilly January night and made her way across Pennsylvania Avenue to the J. Edgar Hoover FBI Building, she was dressed in comfortable jeans, which she customarily wore when she was not in court. Only 5-foot-2-inches tall, she nevertheless cast a formidable figure—a fifty-five-year-old woman with the propulsive gait of someone who couldn't wait to get where she was going.

In recent weeks, pressure had mounted on the FBI to wrap up its investigation. TV talking heads, columnists, and bloggers— liberals and conservatives alike—complained that the investigation was playing havoc with the presidential campaign.

Under pressure, some harsh words had been exchanged between the Justice Department and the FBI. But Shapiro and Comey had managed to maintain a smooth working relationship.

That is, until now.

Recently, Comey had noticed a dramatic change in Shapiro's attitude. According to several sources close to Comey, the FBI director suspected that a new set of marching orders had come down from the White House to the attorney general and her staff. Prosecutors like Betsy Shapiro, who had previously been cooperative, had suddenly begun to impede the investigation.

———

Betsy Shapiro was among the no-indictment crowd from the beginning.

She and Hillary had a relationship that went back more than twenty years. With Hillary's stamp of approval, President Bill Clinton had appointed Shapiro to her civil service job as a Justice Department prosecutor. Shapiro had gained a measure of notoriety when she served as an adviser to the one-time White House deputy chief of staff Harold Ickes, who was nicknamed "the Garbage Man" for his role in cleaning up the Clintons' messes.

During the Paula Jones sexual harassment lawsuit against Bill Clinton, it was Betsy Shapiro, with Hillary's prodding, who encouraged Ickes to keep mum about what he knew regarding President Clinton's sexual scuffle with Kathleen Willey in the private study of the Oval Office.

Shapiro's reputation as a Democrat loyalist followed her through her career. Now she worked for Loretta Lynch, who was chummy with Valerie Jarrett.

"Loretta's one of my favorite people," Jarrett was often heard to say.

Translated from Washingtonese into plain English, that meant Jarrett was confident she could count on Lynch to do the White House's bidding.

The way Jim Comey saw it, the Justice Department was running out the clock, because the Democratic president had no intention of permitting his attorney general to indict the presumptive Democratic nominee. This put Comey on a collision course with the attorney general.

And so, as Betsy Shapiro hurried toward the hastily arranged meeting in Comey's office, she was braced for the worst. Mistrust and mutual suspicion between the FBI and Justice had reached a tipping point, and the stage was set for a showdown.

CHAPTER
11

Citizen Comey

For this all-important meeting in Comey's office, Shapiro brought along Marcia Berman, her feisty assistant at Justice. Though Comey didn't know it, Berman, too, was a liberal Democrat and an ardent Obama supporter. According to the records of the Federal Election Commission, she had contributed to Barack Obama's 2012 campaign for reelection.

As the two women approached the FBI building, they could see it had fallen into a state of disrepair. Chunks of concrete had broken loose from the façade and plunged into protective netting that was meant to shield pedestrians walking on the street below.

Inside, carpets were tattered, paint was peeling, walls were spider-webbed with cracks, and systems designed in the 1960s and 1970s—pneumatic tubes and conveyor belts to handle snail mail and paper files—were woefully out of date. Even the fire alarm worked only sporadically and was in need of repair. America's premier crime-fighting organization was physically falling apart.

When Shapiro and Berman entered Comey's large, L-shaped office, they found the director huddled with his deputies. The 6-foot-8 Comey towered over the petite Shapiro and everyone else in the room.

Under the glass on Comey's desk was a copy of a 1963 letter signed by then Attorney General Robert Kennedy authorizing J. Edgar Hoover to wiretap the telephone conversations of the Reverend Martin Luther King Jr. Comey kept the letter in plain sight, he explained to his aides, as a warning "of the bureau's capacity to do wrong."

He may have had another motive. Hoover was still a highly controversial figure, forty-three years after his death, and Comey—a fiercely competitive and driven man with an outsized ego—hoped that when the decrepit FBI building was eventually torn down and replaced, it would be named the James Brien Comey FBI Building.

Shelves to the right of Comey's desk displayed photos of his wife Patrice and their five children. Nearby, Comey had mounted a slab of concrete that had fallen from the FBI building—a symbol of the fragile nature of political institutions and the reputations of those who ran them.

Comey first rose to prominence back in the 1980s when, as a United States attorney for the Southern District of New York, he prosecuted the billionaire fugitive Marc Rich, who had illegally traded oil with Iran's Ayatollah Khomeini while that country held fifty-two Americans hostage. After President Clinton granted Rich a controversial pardon—the most widely condemned official act of his political career—Comey told a congressional committee, "I was stunned." Comey learned that politics can trump justice.

Comey was also the main prosecutor in Martha Stewart's 2004 conviction for obstruction of justice. Interviewed at the time by the *Observer*'s Alexandra Wolfe, Comey explained the difficulties of prosecuting white-collar crime with words that could apply just as well to the Hillary email investigation nearly twenty years later.

"As I have said a number of times," Comey remarked, "e-mail was the 20th century's greatest gift to law enforcement, because it never goes away, despite what people think."

The episode for which Comey received the loudest kudos occurred when he was the deputy U.S. attorney general during the George W. Bush administration and opposed the use of the so-called "warrantless wiretapping" program. Ever since, conservatives have argued that the liberal mainstream media wrongly gave Comey credit for something he shouldn't have done—damaging a program that was vital to America's national security.

"The left cast the then deputy attorney general as a hero, breathlessly relating how he had rushed to the hospital bedside of then Attorney General John Ashcroft to oppose the reauthorization of the program," wrote the *Wall Street Journal*'s Kimberley A. Strassel. "Mr. Obama, in choosing Mr. Comey [as FBI director], furthered this lore, feting him as a man who 'was prepared to give up a job he loved rather than be part of something he felt was fundamentally wrong.'

"Yet there was nothing tough or bold about opposing a program that was always going to be explosively controversial," Strassel continued. "Intervening wasn't brave; it's what any watch-your-own-backside official would do. There was nothing courageous in later spinning his role, or tarnishing well-meaning government lawyers whose interpretations of the policy differed from his own. Tough would have been standing behind a program that was vital in the war on terror; tough would have been defending the policy when it became a lightning rod for liberal and media criticism."

Like many prosecutors, Comey is a deeply religious man who believes that he is doing God's work—not just metaphorically, but literally. He is an Evangelical Catholic who attends church several times a week. He has said that his faith was put to the test when his nine-day-old son, Collin, died as a result of an undetected bacterial infection that could have been easily treated.

"It's simply not fair to say [my son's death was] God's will," Comey told Chris Smith, a writer for *New York* magazine. "That's inconsistent with any notion of a caring being. What we can say, as Job said, basically, is that we almost can't ask the question of why, but we know what our obligation is: to make some good come of this. Not to say, 'Oh, yeah, yeah, it was worth it that my son died,' or that all of these people died on September 11, or that millions and millions were slaughtered in the Holocaust and in Rwanda. But simply that it is our obligation as people not to let evil hold the field. Not to let bad win."

■■■■

Comey teaches Sunday school, and prays each night with his children before he puts them to bed. After they are tucked in, he always says a prayer for Collin.

On many nights, he shoots hoops in a lighted basketball court in his backyard. When he is finished, his wife Pat usually comes out with a towel and a D.C. Brau beer.

On weekends, he plays squash and basketball with friends. He is a big fan of the New York Knicks and goes to Washington Redskins games when he can find the time.

As FBI director, Comey makes $178,700, but he is financially independent. Before taking the FBI job, he was general counsel of Bridgewater Associates, one of the largest hedge funds in the world. He was paid a lot of money, and walked away with a $3 million severance package.

Friends say that if Comey's legal career hadn't worked out, he probably would have become a stand-up comic or at least a comedy writer. As a court litigator, he was famous for his biting wit. He once asked a defendant, "You don't have to tell me exactly, but approximately how long did it take you to concoct that story?" The defense objected, but the jury got the point.

"He manages to see comedy in even the grimmest legal situations," said a colleague. "I think his sense of humor has gotten him through a lot of tough spots in his life."

▬▬▬

During the months I spent writing this book and trying to get a fix on Comey, I was reminded of the plot of *Citizen Kane*, where a reporter named Jerry Thompson interviews Kane's friends and associates, who draw a sometimes conflicting, sometimes overlapping portrait of a complex man. Here are two interviews that sum up what I found out about James Comey:

Interview One

"To understand 'Big Jim,' as his friends call him, you have to know a bit of background," one of his closest friends said. "At [the College of] William and Mary, he majored in chemistry and religion. He wrote his senior thesis on Reinhold Niebuhr [the author of *Moral Man and Immoral Society*] and Jerry Falwell [co-founder of the Moral Majority]. He became friends with Falwell and was influenced by his evangelism.

"Big Jim sees the world in very strict terms," his friend continued. "He doesn't accept that Hillary and Bill make mistakes, or are sloppy in their methods. He believes they are evil. There is a sexual component to Bill that Jim finds disgraceful and sinful. Hillary compromising national security, endangering the lives of people who are laying down their lives for America—he sees as evil and sinful.

"He thinks the Clintons need to be severely punished for their sins, and he is never going to back down. When Big Jim talks about his case against the Clintons, it is with something of an evangelical fervor. He truly believes he was put in his position as director [of the FBI] for a higher purpose: to see that justice is done no matter the opposition or the odds."

Interview Two

"Jim is incredibly focused on making himself famous," said a former U.S. deputy attorney general, who worked with Comey at the Justice Department. "J. Edgar Hoover made his name by nabbing John Dillinger [the famous Depression-era bank robber]; Jim has always seen Hillary as his John Dillinger.

"Jim's a very bright guy and has a sharp legal mind—I'll give him that," he continued. "He also has a very quick wit. He uses it in discussions with peers, underlings, and his bosses. He can cut to the quick with a sharp remark and really humiliate people. Then, when he sees they are injured by his remarks, he doesn't seem to have any empathy.

"He does that in meetings, in court, and over a beer. That is just the way he is. He hurts people and thinks it's funny. He has always struck me as a big bully."

CHAPTER
12

Stacking Up the Evidence

coffee pot was wheeled into the office, and Betsy Shapiro and Marcia Berman took their places around Comey's conference table, which was set at an angle to his desk. Comey's team included Deputy Director Mark Giuliano, the second highest-ranking official at the FBI; Andrew McCabe, who was in line to succeed Giuliano when he retired; and Chief of Staff Jim Rybicki.

Though Comey was known for his biting sense of humor, he was all business when he conducted meetings in his office. He began by leafing through a stack of yellow legal pads. Then, according to a former Justice Department official who later spoke to Betsy Shapiro, Comey did something that stunned her. He handed the yellow legal pads to an assistant, who sat in front of a computer, and instructed the assistant to enter his notes into the computer and draft more than a dozen potential criminal indictments against Hillary.

Comey explained that he wanted to see in writing how the evidence against Hillary stacked up. The FBI was investigating a number of possible federal crimes that Hillary might have committed, but it was concentrating its efforts on answering three major questions:

1. Was Hillary guilty of "gross negligence" in the handling of national security secrets, which, regardless of intent, was a crime under the Espionage Act?
2. Was Hillary guilty of "public corruption" by offering foreign governments and businessmen favors in return for donations to the Clinton Foundation?
3. Did Hillary lie to the FBI or conspire to suborn witnesses, which was a federal crime?

"Betsy said the information in the drafts would never fly with [Attorney General] Lynch," noted a source who spoke to one of the FBI officials who attended the meeting. "She said the evidence compiled by Comey's battalions of FBI agents proved that Hillary had been sloppy and careless, but it fell far short of proving that her conduct was criminal.

"But Jim wasn't buying that line," the source continued. "He went on at great length about the solid nature of the evidence unearthed by his agents. He believed the FBI was nearing a point where it could refer strong, winnable cases to the Justice Department.

"The debate went on for several hours. Jim never raised his voice or made threats. But he let Betsy know he wasn't going to stand for anyone obstructing the investigation—not the Clintons, not the Justice Department, and not the White House.

"If Loretta Lynch, acting on orders from President Obama, tried to sabotage the FBI investigation, Jim had other avenues he could pursue. For instance, he could circumvent the Justice Department altogether and ask Preet Bharara [the U.S. attorney for the Southern District of New York] to take the case to a judge and ask the judge to empanel a grand jury." (Bharara's jurisdiction extended to Chappaqua, New York, where Hillary had stashed her home brew email server.) "Or," the source added, "Jim could resign and take a bunch of his top lieutenants with him."

Betsy wasn't easily intimidated. She seriously doubted that Comey would resign. He loved his job as director too much. And so, she stuck to her guns: she believed the evidence unearthed so far didn't justify criminal charges against Hillary. Period. Full stop.

It was about two o'clock in the morning when the meeting broke up. Grim-faced, Shapiro and Berman got up to go.

After they left, one of Comey's deputies turned to him and said: "Well, Jim, you've taken on the Justice Department and the White House. What happens next?"

PART 5

THE

INVESTIGATION

We are a fact-gathering organization only. We don't clear anybody. We don't condemn anybody.

—J. Edgar Hoover

CHAPTER 17

The Clinton Brand

fterward, nobody at Bill Clinton's Harlem headquarters could remember the name of the caller, only that it was one of the Justice Department prosecutors handling the Hillary email investigation.

Would the former president be willing to meet with an FBI agent and a prosecutor, the caller wanted to know. *The meeting would be to clarify some issues regarding his wife's email server.*

Bill was in his home office in Chappaqua, taking a nap, when he was awakened by a call from an aide in Harlem, who told him about the prosecutor's request.

"The aide explained that the request had been made in a very respectful way, but Bill went berserk," said a close family friend who was with Bill in Chappaqua at the time. "He blew a gasket. He slammed down the phone and told me that he would never in a million years clarify anything. He would never allow an FBI agent anywhere near him."

Bill called Hillary, who was in Idaho, and berated her for placing him in a compromising position, according to his friend. He blamed Huma Abedin and Cheryl Mills, Hillary's longtime aide, for allowing Hillary to use an unsecure private email system in the first place, then for mishandling the public relations when the news broke, and finally for undermining the Ozymandian empire that Bill had built since leaving the White House, especially his beloved foundation.

The foundation was running into enough trouble as it was. The *New York Times* had done an exposé of the foundation's finances, and Peter Schweizer's bestselling book *Clinton Cash* was being made into a movie that portrayed the foundation as a Clinton family slush fund.

Bill had invited Pope Francis, Leonardo DiCaprio, and many other famous people to the foundation's annual get-together in New York City. But *Politico*'s Kenneth P. Vogel and Noah Weiland reported that "those invitations were among the dozens turned down by all manner of celebrities, dignitaries and donors…who said the controversies swirling around the foundation and Hillary Clinton's presidential campaign have made some bold-faced names and donors wary of the foundation."

"Bill yelled at Hillary until he was hoarse," the friend recalled. "He said that no matter what happened with the FBI investigation, he and Hillary would be harassed over this problem for years to come.

"'Even if you're elected president,' he said, 'there are groups like Judicial Watch and news organizations all over the country that will file suits and FOIA requests, and they'll never give up.'

"He said their enemies would be investigating everything they did. There would be hearings and legal bills running into the millions of dollars.

"'The lawsuits will haunt your presidency,' he told her.

"By the time he hung up the phone, he was utterly exhausted. His face was the color of ashes. He collapsed back in bed. He looked like a very, very old man."

———

It was no exaggeration to say that Bill Clinton was a dying man.

His cardiologist had told him there was nothing he could do to reverse Bill's progressive heart disease, and Bill frequently talked about his mortality. He told friends that he didn't think he had long to live. Maybe not even long enough to see Hillary through her first term in the White House. He had made plans for his state funeral, and had recently redrawn his will to include his grandchildren (Chelsea was pregnant with her second child).

It was becoming harder for him to accomplish the most basic daily tasks—getting in and out of chairs, walking without stumbling, shaking hands without trembling, speaking above a hoarse whisper.

His problems weren't only physical. His mental faculties were deteriorating as well. Once a silver-tongued orator, he frequently was at a loss for words. Just as often, he misspoke and said the opposite of what he meant.

His temperament and personality—his very nature—were all changing. The man whom Charlie Rose called "the best political animal that's ever been in American politics" told friends he didn't have "the fire in my belly" for another campaign.

"Campaigns today are harder, tougher, and more grueling than they were in my day," he said. "It's a young man's sport, and I'm definitely not young any more. And I don't feel the anger you need to keep going."

What made matters worse was that he fundamentally disagreed with Hillary on a host of key political issues.

"Hillary buys all that left-wing stuff that she talks about when she's on the campaign trail," his friend said. "At heart, she's never changed. She's the same old Wellesley College radical. But Bill is still a guy who is for small, efficient government and for incentives to get people off welfare. He doesn't want to use taxes as a means of redistributing wealth. He didn't think that was a good idea when he was president, and he doesn't think it is now.

"The point is, Bill finds it hard to preach what he doesn't believe. Sure, he can bullshit like any other politician, but it doesn't come off as convincing as it would if he actually believed it."

Many Democrats (who were apparently afflicted with amnesia about Whitewater, Monica Lewinsky, and eleventh-hour pardons) looked back on Bill's years in the White House as a golden age. To them, it was a time of peace and prosperity. Hillary exploited those memories; she tried to sell people on the idea that they would get a third Bill Clinton term if they elected her.

"My husband…I'm going to put in charge of revitalizing the economy because, you know, he knows how to do it," Hillary promised primary voters in Kentucky. "I've already told my husband that if I'm so fortunate enough to be president and he will be the first gentleman, I'll expect him to go to work…to get incomes rising."

Her vow to bring back the good old days—when the Clintons promised voters that they were getting two for the price of one—struck some observers as curious, to say the least.

"Mrs. Clinton's remarks are a revealing turn, not least because so far she's been running for President Obama's third term," the *Wall Street Journal* editorialized. "But since Democrats seem to agree that the economic status quo is dismal, and thus they can't run on Mr. Obama's record, the presumptive nominee is trying to confuse voters with halcyon memories of the 1990s boom."

Donald Trump, the Republican nominee, put it more succinctly: "Hillary wants Bill around the White House so she can keep an eye on him."

When reporters asked Bill to explain the role he played in his wife's campaign, he had a pat answer: he did whatever she asked him to do. But when the reporters weren't around, and he was alone with friends, he admitted he was ambivalent about the whole Hillary enterprise.

"I feel like the dog chasing the car that doesn't really want to catch it," he said, according to a close friend. "I don't need the scrutiny of being in the White House. I love my life the way it is. I don't want reporters up my ass all the time. I couldn't be chasing skirts in the White House. They can't impeach me again, but it would be very bad for Hillary.

"Believe me, if Hillary wins" he added, "I'm going to stay as far away from the White House as possible."

▄▄▄▄

In the meantime, Bill assembled a team of lawyers to advise him about the FBI investigation and, more important from his point of view, the ramifications for the Clinton Brand.

The FBI investigation threatened not only Hillary's future, but Bill's as well—whether he could continue on with his foundation, his speeches, his money-grubbing, his hobnobbing with the high and mighty, his travels in private jets, and his fun and games with the young interns in the Clinton Library.

His lawyers addressed a troubling statement made by Michael Mukasey, who served as an attorney general under President George W. Bush. Mukasey wrote an op-ed declaring that if Hillary were convicted under 18 U.S. Code § 2071—the federal law forbidding the concealment or destruction of documents, which is a felony—she would be ineligible to become president, because the statute bars those convicted of it from holding government office.

Bill's legal experts disagreed, because the Constitution sets the qualifications for the office of the president, and the Constitution does not mention 18 U.S. Code § 2071. Mukasey withdrew his claim and admitted his error. Nevertheless, it was true that if convicted, and if she won the election, Hillary Clinton would be not only the first woman but the first convicted felon to be president of the United States.

One of Hillary's most outspoken advocates was Anne Tompkins, the former U.S. attorney for the Western District of North Carolina, who handled the case that brought down David Petraeus, the former director of the CIA. Tompkins argued that the four-star general knowingly engaged in criminal conduct by sharing classified material with his mistress. Hillary's conduct, Tompkins said, did not rise to that level of wrongdoing.

There were several problems with Tompkins and her argument. First, Tompkins was hardly an unbiased expert; she was a registered Democrat and a Hillary donor. Second, Petraeus was not found guilty of *criminal* conduct; he was permitted to plead guilty to a single *misdemeanor* count. And third, as Andrew McCarthy, a former assistant U.S. attorney for the Southern District of New York, pointed out in *PJ Media*, "Tompkins never had anything to do with the Clinton investigation; and she can't possibly know the full extent of the FBI's evidence because the probe is ongoing and, quite properly, the FBI is not commenting publicly."

Next, Bill's attorneys examined the opinion of David Metcalfe, who, for three years, had been in charge of the Department of Justice's records storage regulations. Metcalfe came up with an unexpected twist: Yes, Hillary could be charged with the improper disposal of government records, he said, but that didn't matter. Once an employee left his or her government post, no formal charges could be brought against them.

The most serious challenge, as far as Bill's lawyers were concerned, came from David C. Keesler, the United States magistrate judge for the Western District of North Carolina. Keesler had been in charge of the Petraeus case. He doubled the fine the prosecutors recommended, from $50,000 to $100,000, and sentenced Petraeus to two years of probation. Keesler was now looking into charges by the inspector general of the intelligence community that many top-secret documents had passed through Hillary's email system. Keesler was a hard-ass judge and a major threat to Hillary.

The best outcome for Hillary and Bill, his lawyers agreed, would be if Obama appointed a special counsel to handle the email investigation, thereby taking the case out of the hands of his attorney general and avoiding the appearance of White House obstructionism. To prove that he was nonpartisan, Obama would almost certainly appoint a Republican, which would be good for the Clintons, because then they could claim that the investigation was a right-wing conspiracy. Even more important, a special counsel would take years to finish the job, by which time Hillary would be in the second or third year of her presidency.

At that point, Bill's lawyers said only half-joking, Hillary could pardon herself.

CHAPTER
14

Pay to Play

"I got a heads-up from my attorney that the FBI wanted to interview me about Hillary, and specifically about her conflict of interest handling Clinton Foundation business while she was running the nation's foreign policy."

The speaker was a retired Foreign Service officer who had worked closely with Hillary and flown with her on several State Department missions overseas. This former diplomat was quoted in my book *Unlikeable: The Problem with Hillary*; she said she had witnessed Hillary dealing with Clinton Foundation and Clinton Global Initiative business from her office and conference room on the seventh floor of the State Department, and from the cabin of Air Force Two.

"Knowing what I knew, I guess I wasn't really surprised to be contacted by the FBI," the source said in an interview for this book.* "I'm a Democrat and supporter of Hillary for president, but I was deeply resentful that she carried out her family foundation business so openly when she was at State. It was as though being secretary of state was her part-time job, while her first priorities were raising money for her presidential run, which she was planning from day one, and raising money for the Clinton Foundation.

"The amazing thing about how she behaved was that she was completely unembarrassed that the people who worked with her knew what she was doing," the source continued. "She had no qualms, because she said that the work she did at State and the work she was doing for the foundation and the Global Initiative were related and complemented each other.

"When I flew on her plane, she always took along a bunch of manila folders marked CF and CGI—the Clinton Foundation and the Clinton Global Initiative. The folders had dividers labeled Donations, Fund Raising, AIDS/HIV, Haiti, and so on. There was no question what she was up to."

After the veteran Foreign Service officer retired, she returned home to Chicago, and it was there that the FBI interview took place.

---

* The source was interviewed twenty-one times.

"I was asked if I preferred the agents to visit at my business or come down to their field office. I didn't have an office in the city, and I sure as hell didn't want those FBI agents, with their dark suits, white shirts, and dark ties, showing up at my apartment and spooking my neighbors, because it might look like I was being arrested or something.

"I consulted with a judge, a longtime friend of mine, and asked him what I should do. He said words to the effect, 'Tell the truth but don't volunteer anything.'

"So I took an Uber out to the near West Side to the FBI office on West Roosevelt Road in Chicago. It's a grim, forbidding ten-story building. And I turned myself in [laughs].

"My friend the judge had given me good advice, but it was easier for him to offer it than for me to carry it out, because the so-called interview was more like an interrogation. Every time I answered a question, the agents peppered me with ten more. I half expected the third-degree spotlight to be shined in my eyes [laughs again].

"I came away with the impression, after ninety minutes of grilling, that the FBI was going after this case with a vengeance."

Orders had come down from James Comey that it was time to expand the FBI investigation from Hillary's mishandling of classified emails to her unethical—and almost certainly illegal—mingling of State Department and Clinton Foundation business. The FBI director believed that Hillary had dispensed favors to foreign governments and businessmen who contributed money to the Clinton Foundation.

In common parlance, that was called pay to play.

Comey's suspicions about the Clintons' dodgy methods weren't anything new. As *Time* magazine's deputy Washington bureau chief, Massimo Calabresi, reported, when Comey was deputy special counsel to the Senate Whitewater Committee in the 1990s, he came to "some damning conclusions: Hillary Clinton was personally involved in mishandling documents and had ordered others to block investigators as they pursued their case.

"Worse," Calabresi continued, "her behavior fit into a pattern of concealment: she and her husband had tried to hide their roles in two other matters under investigation by law enforcement. Taken together, the interference by White House officials, which included destruction of documents, amounted to 'far more than just aggressive lawyering or political naiveté,' Comey and his fellow investigators concluded. It constituted 'a highly improper pattern of deliberate misconduct.'"

Now, if Hillary were found guilty of pay to play while she was secretary of state, she could be charged under several different statutes. Among them: the federal official bribery and gratuity statute, 18 U.S.C. § 201 (enacted 1962); the Foreign Corrupt Practices Act (enacted 1977); and the federal program bribery statute, 18 U.S.C. § 666 (enacted 1984).

Comey wasn't the only one who believed there was a mountain of evidence to prove Hillary had violated public corruption laws. In an article for RealClearPolitics titled "Hillary Clinton's

Coming Legal Crisis," Charles Lipson, the Peter B. Ritzma pro-
fessor of Political Science and the founder and director of the
Program on International Politics, Economics and Security at the
University of Chicago, wrote:

> Major donors to the foundation often had business
> before the State Department, and they sometimes
> received help. After the devastating 2010 earthquake in
> Haiti, for instance, Bill Clinton was named co-chair-
> man of the Interim Haiti Recovery Commission, and,
> according to the *Wall Street Journal*, "the State Depart-
> ment began directing parties interested in competing
> for Haiti contracts to the Clinton Foundation." Not
> surprisingly, many contractors became foundation
> donors, or were already. The FBI now has to decide if
> any of this was a "pay to play" arrangement.

Evidence of other pay-to-play scandals abounded. I described
several of them in *Unlikeable: The Problem with Hillary.*

The Electric-Car Connection: While Hillary was secretary of
state, her younger brother Tony Rodham received special favors from
the U.S. government for an electric car company owned by an old
Clinton crony, Terry McAuliffe, the current governor of Virginia.

The Haiti Connection: While his sister was secretary of state,
Tony Rodham was appointed to the advisory board of VCS Mining, a U.S.-based company that received a gold-mining contract
in Haiti.

The Nigerian Connection: A Lebanese-Nigerian billionaire, who was one of the Clinton Foundation's biggest donors, lobbied Hillary not to designate the al-Qaeda–linked Nigerian Islamist group Boko Haram as a terrorist organization. As long as she was at Foggy Bottom, the murderous Boko Haram stayed off the official U.S. terrorist list.

The Canadian Connection: A Canadian businessman who donated millions of dollars to the Clinton Foundation was granted permission to sell control of 20 percent of the U.S. uranium production capacity to Vladimir Putin's Russia. Putin showed his gratitude by inviting Bill Clinton to give a speech in Moscow, for which he was paid $500,000.

The UBS Connection: While she was secretary of state, Hillary intervened on behalf of UBS, a giant of the Swiss banking industry that had donated $600,000 to the Clinton Foundation and paid Bill Clinton $1.5 million for a series of speeches.

In addition to these examples of pay-to-play scandals, here are three that didn't make the cut at the time *Unlikeable* was published.

The TD Bank Connection: "TD Bank never engaged Bill Clinton to speak during his first eight years out of the White House," noted Betsy McCaughey, a senior fellow at the London Center for Policy Research. "But in 2009, four days after Hillary was nominated secretary of state, Bill made the first of a string of speeches for which TD paid almost $2 million." TD Bank was the largest investor in the Keystone XL pipeline, a project that, because it crossed the border between Canada and the United States, needed approval from the State Department. Hillary did not take a public position on the pipeline until more than two years after she left the State Department. She was then on the campaign trail in Iowa and needed to shore up her support among left-wing environmentalists. She finally said, in September 2015, that she opposed the pipeline as "a distraction from important work we have to do on climate change."

The Boeing Connection: While she was secretary of state, Hillary helped Boeing win a $35 billion Air Force tanker-refueling contract. After the Air Force deal, Boeing demonstrated its gratitude by donating $900,000 to the Clinton Foundation and paying former President Bill Clinton $450,000 for two speeches.

The Energy Pioneer Solutions Connection: Bill Clinton helped direct nearly $3 million to an energy company that was owned in part by a "family friend" who was rumored to be his mistress. Part of that money came in the form of a federal Department of Energy grant he helped arrange. The rest came from an investment made at a Clinton Global Initiative conference. Chuck Ross of the *Daily Caller* reported that the Clinton Global Initiative "scrubbed its website of evidence of a $2 million commitment that Clinton helped arrange for the company, Energy Pioneer Solutions, in order to avoid drawing attention to the former president's friendship with that investor, a 56-year-old blonde divorcee named Julie Tauber McMahon.... Some outlets have alleged that McMahon, who is a neighbor of the Clintons in Chappaqua, N.Y., is the Bill Clinton friend nicknamed [by the Secret Service] 'Energizer'...[who reportedly] visited the Clinton home frequently but timed her stops when Hillary Clinton was not there."

That Hillary ran a pay-to-play State Department was well known in Washington. But no one had done a thing about it—until, maybe, now.

———

"The FBI agents asked me a few questions about the email situation, but they didn't linger on it," the former Foreign Service officer recalled about her interrogation. "They wanted to know if I was aware Hillary used a private server and for how long I knew. The answer was from day one, when she became secretary.

"They asked if I was aware some documents sent were classified," the source continued. "I said I didn't recall, but some undoubtedly carried some level of classification. I was sure from the way they questioned me that they had copies of all the emails exchanged between Hillary and me. It seemed to me that they had already cracked the email case, and were eager to move on.

"Then they zeroed in on how many times and where I had seen Hillary working on foundation business at State. I said that the occasions were too numerous to mention. Under their questioning, I agreed that it was an almost daily occurrence, and I told them that there were always a pile of foundation folders and financial materials on her desk, and on her Air Force plane, or carried by Huma wherever Hillary went.

"In the end, the agents were polite and they walked me out. They asked if I would come back again if needed. Obviously, I agreed, but I sure hope it doesn't happen."

CHAPTER
15

"The General Has Arrived"

"The Capital Grille is as manly a steakhouse as you can picture, from the dark wood to the stuffed animal heads to side dishes that arrive in small barges (nutmeg-laced creamed spinach)," wrote Tom Sietsema, the *Washington Post*'s restaurant critic.

The only thing Sietsema failed to describe in his review were the "manly" regular customers—FBI agents packing heat, and tough-talking Justice Department prosecutors in dark power suits. The Capital Grille was their hangout, and on weekend nights they gathered round its semicircular bar. They noshed on chilled shrimp and grilled lollipop lamb chops, bought each other shots of single malt Scotch, and argued in loud voices above the din of the crowd about the Clinton email investigation.

The views of the two sides—the agents and the prosecutors—sometimes overlapped. Many agreed that the investigation was proceeding at a snail's pace, and that if the target of the probe had been a congressman or senator instead of Hillary Clinton, the presumptive Democratic presidential nominee, indictments would have been handed down a long time ago.

Several prosecutors, who were in sympathy with Hillary's politics, admitted they were appalled at the outrageous liberties she had taken with classified material. The nation's most secret documents called Special Access Program (SAP) had passed through Hillary's unsecure email system, endangering the United States' intelligence gathering methods and the identity of American spies.

"She was a major player in the White House, a senator, and the secretary of state," said one of the prosecutors. "She knew what was classified and what was not from a mile away, whether it was marked classified or not."

"She was briefed and signed an official affidavit that she understood how to handle classified material," said another prosecutor. "Apparently, she didn't give a flying fuck."

"If you go by the letter of the law, she broke several of them," said an agent.

"Yeah, but no jury's going to convict the nominee of the Democratic Party without proof that she acted with criminal intent," said a prosecutor. "And that just ain't going to happen."

"What about Title 18?" one of the agents asked.

He was referring to 18 U.S.C. § 1001, which prohibited knowingly and willingly making false or fraudulent statements, or concealing information. Many agents believed that Hillary and her top aides—Huma Abedin, Cheryl Mills, and Jake Sullivan—had misled the FBI by making materially false statements, which was punishable by a stiff fine and several years in jail.

"Dennis Hastert [the former speaker of the House], Rod Blagojevich [the former governor of Illinois], and Martha Stewart were all sent to jail for lying to the FBI," an agent pointed out.

"But Hillary isn't Martha Stewart," a prosecutor replied. "She doesn't write cookbooks and give tips on entertaining. She's the next fucking president of the United States."

"Not if we can help it," a slightly inebriated FBI agent said.

On this particular Friday night, the agents and the prosecutors were packed three deep at the bar when there was a sudden rustle of activity at the front door. A flying wedge of Secret Service agents entered the room with Attorney General Loretta Lynch and her aides.

"The General has arrived," said one of the bartenders.

The media had hung the nickname "the General" on attorneys general of the United States ever since Janet Reno held the post. Reno earned the nickname in part because of her imposing stature—she was 6-foot-2-inches tall—and in part because of her role in the FBI's disastrous 1993 attack on the Branch Davidians' compound in Waco, Texas, which Reno approved and which resulted in the deaths of four government agents and six Branch Davidians.

The barroom crowd parted for Lynch and her aides as they made their way to a table in the dining area. The Secret Service detail kept watch from a nearby table.

Cocktails, appetizers, and main courses all appeared on Lynch's table without a word from her or her aides. Apparently, everything had been ordered in advance, or the chef was familiar with the General's palate.

If anyone strayed near her table, the Secret Service shooed them away. But at one point, Lynch spotted an old friend, a judge with wide-ranging political connections, who was standing in the barroom schmoozing with agents and prosecutors, and she waved to him.

He went over to her table.

She nodded to the Secret Service agents that he was okay, but she didn't get up to greet him.

███

Lynch had not been Obama's first choice to succeed the controversial Eric Holder, who as attorney general had used a liberal litmus test to decide which laws he chose to enforce and which ones he chose to ignore. Holder and his wife were close personal friends of Barack and Michelle Obama, and Obama had allowed him to stay in his job long after he was held in contempt of Congress. Holder had been found guilty of stonewalling the investigation into Operation Fast and Furious in which federal agents sold weapons to gun dealers in the hope of tracking them to Mexican drug cartels. A U.S. Immigration and Customs Enforcement agent and several hundred Mexicans died as a result of the fatally flawed sting operation.

Obama wanted to replace Holder with another favorite, Kathryn Ruemmler, the White House Counsel, who had given the president legal cover to issue scores of executive orders that many legal scholars found blatantly unconstitutional. Ruemmler withdrew her name when it became apparent that the Republican-controlled Senate wouldn't confirm her.

With Ruemmler out of the running, Loretta Lynch's name rose to the top of Obama's short list. She was a "two-fer"—an African American and a woman, as well as a prominent prosecutor. Lynch came highly recommended by the Reverend Al Sharpton. Over the years, Sharpton had managed to lose weight (he went from 305 pounds to 138) and shed his reputation (at least in liberal quarters) as a rabble-rousing con artist. When Lynch was the United States attorney for the Eastern District of New York, she befriended Sharpton, who had become the Obama White House's go-to guy for issues related to black America.

Sharpton wasn't shy about using his leverage when it came to appointing a new attorney general.

"We are engaged in immediate conversations with the White House on deliberations over a successor whom we hope will continue in the general direction of Attorney General Holder," he said.

Sharpton gave his blessing to Lynch. Her nomination process dragged on for 166 days, making it one of the longest in U.S. history.

She was finally confirmed as the eighty-third attorney general of the United States on April 23, 2015.

Lynch followed in Eric Holder's hard-left footsteps. She filed a lawsuit against North Carolina over its law that required people to use public bathrooms that matched their actual biological sex, not the "gender" they identified with. And she sued the federal Election Assistant Commission over its decision to allow states to require people to provide IDs when they registered to vote.

"I think that she has shown in an understated way, but with loud ramifications," said Sharpton, "that she is no one who shrinks from the legacy of Robert Kennedy or Eric Holder."

Standing just five feet tall, Lynch was not an imposing figure. She was fourteen inches shorter than Janet Reno, and she and her husband, Stephen Hargrove, who worked at Showtime, did not dine at the White House with the Obamas as had Holder and his obstetrician wife, Dr. Sharon Malone. But in the gathering storm between Barack Obama and FBI Director James Comey, Loretta Lynch was without doubt the president's commanding general.

CHAPTER

16

High Noon in the Oval

You could always tell from the look in his eye when James Comey had his Irish up.

And the FBI director had that killer look right now.

It was January 29, 2016, and an aide had just handed Comey a printout of today's White House press conference by Josh Earnest, the president's spokesman. There, marked for Comey's attention, was Earnest's response to a reporter who had asked whether Hillary Clinton was likely to be indicted as a result of the FBI's investigation into her personal emails.

"Based on what we know from the Department of Justice," Earnest said, "it does not seem to be headed in that direction."

Based on what we know!

"How does Earnest know anything?" Comey asked.

It was a rhetorical question.

Uniformed FBI agents on Attorney General Loretta Lynch's protective detail had informed Comey that Lynch had locked an armful of documents on the FBI investigation into her briefcase and delivered them to the White House. More than once, Lynch had brought along a Justice Department prosecutor who was working on the Hillary case to brief the president's staff.

These briefings between Lynch and the White House (which Lynch publicly denied because they were unethical) had been going on since Comey's investigation began in the summer of 2015. Comey was aware, of course, that his criminal investigation of Hillary Clinton was inevitably linked with the highest possible stakes in American politics. If his agents turned up evidence of criminal wrongdoing on Hillary's part, it would ignite the greatest political firestorm since Watergate. And more likely than not, that would derail Hillary's candidacy for the White House.

But Comey was determined to keep up appearances that he would not be swayed by political considerations. The FBI director's job was to assemble all the facts and make a "referral," or recommendation, to the Justice Department. His say-so carried a lot of weight, but in the end, it was up to Lynch, the nation's chief law enforcement officer, to make the call whether to indict.

And Comey had reason to fear that the outcome was controlled by political forces beyond his control.

It was one of the great ironies of present-day politics that Barack Obama, who viewed the Clintons as his implacable enemy, was now eager to give Hillary a Get Out of Jail Free card, and that his potential opponent to doing this was the man Barack Obama himself had appointed director of the FBI.

Nothing had changed about Obama's feelings toward the Clintons: he still couldn't stomach Bill, and he could barely tolerate Hillary. But he was stuck with Hillary as his party's presidential nominee, and whether he liked it or not, he had to call a truce to their blood feud.

The alternative was unthinkable.

If Hillary was indicted, it would convulse the entire political system, monopolize media coverage, and wreck Obama's final months in office. Even if Hillary hung on and ran for president while under indictment (which she was privately vowing to do), she would almost certainly go down to defeat. A Republican would waltz into the White House. A Republican president, with a complaisant Republican Congress, could undo all of Obama's signature achievements—Obamacare, the Iran nuclear deal, and hundreds of Obama's executive orders.

To avoid that nightmare scenario, Obama had been doing his best to defend Hillary and her indefensible use of an unsecure and easily hackable email system. Back in October 2015, in an interview with Steve Kroft of *60 Minutes*, he underplayed the consequences of Hillary's action.

"This," said Obama, "is not a situation in which America's national security was endangered."

At the time, Comey was outraged by those remarks, but he chose not to complain directly to Obama. Instead, he fired a shot across Obama's bow. He told a congressional committee that since *he* wasn't briefing the Obama administration, and since only *he* knew all the facts about the FBI investigation, the president of the United States *didn't know what he was talking about.*

"I hope the American people know the FBI well enough and the nature and character of this organization," Comey told the Senate panel. "As I've said many times, we don't give a rip about politics."

But today's press conference by Josh Earnest was a game changer. Earnest had let the cat out of the bag when he said, *"Based on what we know from the Department of Justice...."*

It was a public admission that the White House and the Justice Department were working in cahoots. They weren't even trying to hide their collusion. They were rubbing Comey's nose in it. And given "Big Jim's" essential nature—proud, ambitious, moralizing—he could not let that pass.

He picked up the phone and said, "I want to see the president."

According to multiple sources who were later briefed on the meeting between Comey and Obama, when the FBI director entered the Oval Office, he didn't know what kind of reception he would get.

The president bounded from his desk and greeted Comey warmly. At 6-foot-8, the FBI director had more than a half-foot on the 6-foot-1 president, forcing Obama to look up to meet Comey's eyes. It was common knowledge in Washington that this president did not like to look up to anyone—literally or figuratively.

Obama did a good job hiding his discomfort. He shook Comey's hand, patted him on the back, and led him over to a sofa. From the effusive way he treated Comey, nobody would have guessed that the two men disliked each other.

In fact, they held each other in contempt. Comey complained to his top assistants that in the few encounters he had had with Obama, the president treated him with a tone of condescension. To Obama, the FBI was like any other cop shop, not the premier law enforcement organization in the country.

More important, Comey and Obama were engaged in a war of words over the most sensitive issue on Obama's desk—race relations in America.

"White House officials were said to be livid about a speech that Mr. Comey gave…in which he said the increase in crime in big cities this year might be a result of police officers' concern about getting out of their patrol cars because their interactions with [African Americans] could be caught on video," the *Washington Times* reported. "Mr. Comey also appeared to dispute the administration's view that the imprisonment of thousands of criminals in the 1980s and 1990s during a high-crime era was an example of 'mass incarceration.'"

The president had wanted Valerie Jarrett to sit in on the meeting with Comey. She was both his senior adviser and best friend, and Obama freely admitted he did not make a single decision without first consulting her. But Jarrett felt that her presence would only antagonize the FBI director.

Obama ordered coffee and biscotti, and he and Comey chatted for a few minutes about their families. Then Comey got to the point of the meeting.

He said he understood why people were losing patience with the long-drawn-out FBI investigation. No one wanted to see it over more than he did. But he couldn't be rushed. He couldn't make a referral until his technical specialists had finished retrieving every speck of evidence they could lay their hands on (including, if possible, the thirty-thousand-plus "personal" emails Hillary had erased from her server), and his field agents had completed their interviews, including with members of the intelligence community as well as with Hillary and her closest aides.

Obama nodded gravely, but didn't say anything.

Valerie Jarrett had warned Obama that Comey might resign if Attorney General Lynch refused to issue an indictment, and that a mass resignation by Comey and his top lieutenants could set off a political tornado to rival what followed Watergate's "Saturday Night Massacre."

But Comey did not mention the "R" word.

He didn't have to.

The fact that the director of the Federal Bureau of Investigation was staring down the president of the United States, and implicitly warning him against political interference, was threat enough.

After Comey left, Jarrett slipped into the Oval. The expression on Obama's face told the whole story.

"I've never seen Barack look angrier," she later told a friend.

CHAPTER
17

"Even God Can't Read Them"

J ames Comey had that killer look in his eye again.

The FBI's investigation into Hillary's hazardous email practices had generated some ten thousand pages of reports and analysis—about two and a half million words, or the equivalent of four copies of *War and Peace*—but the Criminal, Cyber, Response, and Services Branch had contributed little to this mountain of evidence. So far, Comey's cyber team had managed to retrieve only a fraction of the 31,000 "personal" emails that Hillary had wiped clean from her server in Chappaqua.

"It's the one area of the Bureau's work that Comey thinks is subpar," said a former Justice Department official who spoke with top FBI officials. "There have been times when the IT technicians have thrown up their hands in despair. Comey ordered the department reshuffled and doubled in size. But he's found it hard to build an army in the middle of a battle."

Clearly, someone on Hillary's staff had gone to extraordinary lengths to make certain that the information wiped from the server would be virtually impossible for the FBI to retrieve.

"[Hillary] and her lawyers had those emails deleted, and they didn't just push the delete button; they had them deleted where even God can't read them," said Trey Gowdy, chairman of the House Select Committee on Benghazi. "They were using something called BleachBit." (A publicly available overwrite algorithm, BleachBit is used to securely erase the contents of computer hard drives to prevent recovery of files.) "You don't use BleachBit for yoga emails or bridesmaids emails. When you're using BleachBit, it is something you really do not want the world to see."

The most likely suspect was Bryan Pagliano, the IT specialist who helped set up Hillary's private email server. When Trey Gowdy's committee subpoenaed Pagliano and ordered him to testify about Hillary's email server, he invoked his Fifth Amendment privilege against self-incrimination. Shortly thereafter, the Justice Department granted Pagliano immunity from criminal prosecution in exchange for his testimony.

Pagliano kept Hillary's computer security logs and knew who had access to her email system. He was aware that hackers in China, Russia, North Korea, Iran, and other countries had attempted to attack Hillary's server. After one such attempt, Hillary's system was shut down and her top aides were warned not to send "anything sensitive" to the secretary of state.

"After another suspicious attempt," reported the *Washington Times*, "Mrs. Clinton said she was scared to open email—but failed to report the matter."

Of all the hackers, the most infamous was Marcel Lehel Lazar, an out-of-work Romanian taxi cab driver who used the Internet moniker Guccifer—a combination of Gucci and Lucifer. Guccifer boasted that he had broken into several American computer accounts—those of the Bush family, Sidney Blumenthal, and Hillary Clinton. The FBI extradited Guccifer to the United States, where he pleaded guilty and gave jailhouse interviews to Fox News and other media outlets.

Guccifer said he had breached Hillary's server and come across evidence that other hackers were also on her server.

"For me, it was easy…easy for me, for everybody," Guccifer told Fox News. "As far as I remember, yes, there were…up to ten, like IPs from other parts of the world."

With Guccifer locked away in a federal prison, Comey launched a worldwide manhunt for others who might have hacked Hillary's email server.

"Jim wanted to track down more hackers wherever they were hiding, get them in custody and bring them back to federal penitentiaries where he could have them interrogated," said a former Justice Department prosecutor. "If he could prove conclusively that hackers, working either on their own or for foreign governments, breached Hillary's email server and acquired America's most vital national secrets, he would have finally got what he'd been looking for all along—the smoking gun."

███

A smoldering gun—if not a smoking one—turned up unexpectedly when Iran's Justice Ministry announced that Shahram Amiri, an Iranian nuclear scientist, had been found guilty of being an American spy and had been hanged for treason. Critics immediately blamed Amiri's death on Hillary, who had discussed Amiri's fate on her unsecure—and easily hackable—email system.

"I'm not going to comment on what [Amiri] may or may not have done for the United States government," Tom Cotton, a member of the Senate Select Committee on Intelligence, said on *Face the Nation*, "but in the emails that were on Hillary Clinton's private server, there were conversations among her senior advisers about this gentleman. That goes to show just how reckless and careless her decision was to put that kind of highly classified information on a private server. And I think her judgment is not suited to keep this country safe."

Conservatives concurred with Cotton.

The *Washington Times* called Amiri's death "the first casualty of Hillary Clinton's server."

"Amiri had given Iranian nuclear secrets to the CIA and used a cover story upon returning to Iran that he had been kidnapped," wrote Abraham H. Miller, emeritus professor of political science at the University of Cincinnati and a distinguished fellow with the Haym Salomon Center. "That story was blown in Hillary Clinton's emails, which referred to Amiri as 'our friend' and discussed his providing information about Iran's nuclear program. ... Iran confirmed his execution and his mother confirmed receiving his body. The State Department is still withholding confirmation, as if anyone cares. The tragedy of Amiri's death is compounded by the immeasurable harm it will do to America's ability to recruit, now and in the future, human assets. A nation's security is often dependent on people willing to take risks that benefit it. The likelihood of that has been greatly diminished by Hillary Clinton's flagrant disregard of the national security consequences of her reckless email use."

PART 6

COUNTERSTRIKE

Thus, what is of supreme importance in war is to attack the enemy's strategy.

—Sun Tzu

CHAPTER
18

Conspiracy of Silence

On a pleasant early spring weekend, James and Patrice Comey invited a group of friends and their children for a barbecue at their home in McLean, Virginia. There were clowns for the kids and beer for the grown-ups. At one point during the party, Comey drew one of his friends aside to a quiet place where they could talk in private.

"Jim and I go back years and years, our wives are friendly, we trust each other implicitly, and he obviously felt the need to get some things off his chest," the friend said in an interview for this book.* "He told me that he had called John Brennan [director of the Central Intelligence Agency] and James Clapper [director of

---

* The source was interviewed nine times.

National Intelligence] and explained to them how important it was that their staffs cooperate with the FBI investigation of Hillary's emails. He wanted to depose the people in the intelligence community who had actually generated the highly classified information that ended up on Hillary's server. Both Brennan and Clapper assured him they would give the FBI their full cooperation.

"But then nothing happened," Comey's friend continued. "In fact, everywhere Jim's agents went—the CIA, the Defense Intelligence Agency, the National Security Agency—they were stonewalled. There was a conspiracy of silence. That couldn't happen without the connivance of the White House. Jim suspected that, in an effort to protect Hillary, either Valerie Jarrett or Denis McDonough [the White House chief of staff] had signaled the heads of the intelligence community to throw up as many obstacles as they could.

"Jim said, 'I've been in government most of my career and I've never seen such obstructionism like this before.'

"The most run-of-the-mill requests from the FBI were ignored. It was clear to Jim that people in the intelligence community were scared shitless of getting on the wrong side of the White House. Rather than help the FBI dig up evidence that Hillary had endangered national security, they were willing to risk the safety of our country to save their necks.

"Jim said that his relationship with the president had deteriorated to the point where the White House actually tried to transfer some personnel from the Justice Department to the FBI, where they would act as moles and report back to Lynch. Jim's internal affairs guys got wind of the White House scheme and prevented several suspicious Justice Department people from being quote loaned unquote to the Bureau."

To assemble evidence that Hillary's email server had been successfully hacked, Comey had to find a way to bypass the White House's cordon sanitaire. In the spring of 2016, he phoned Mireille Ballestrazzi, the head of INTERPOL, the International Criminal Police Organization that facilitated contacts and information among national police forces.

Relations between the FBI and INTERPOL had not always been cordial; in the 1950s, J. Edgar Hoover considered withdrawing the U.S. from membership in INTERPOL, because he felt that it was encroaching on his territory and grabbing headlines.

But Comey had no such reservations about INTERPOL or with Ballestrazzi, the first female president in the organization's history. Famous in France for tracking down stolen art and combating organized crime, Ballestrazzi was the subject of a book called *Madame la commissaire.*

"She is one of the women who are the pride of the French police," said Manuel Valls, the former minister of the Interior and the current premier of France.

In Comey's estimation, Ballestrazzi had several things to recommend her: she was a cyber crime expert; she had opened a Global Complex for Innovation in Singapore to combat cybercrime; and she was dedicated, as she put it, to "global police cooperation."

Shortly after Comey called her, Ballestrazzi alerted investigators in more than one hundred countries to help identify suspects who might have hacked Hillary's email server. She and Comey set up a hotline between their deputies in Washington and Lyon, the headquarters of INTERPOL.

Within a matter of weeks, Ballestrazzi put together a list of people in several European and Middle Eastern countries and China who were suspected of hacking Hillary's email system. Ballestrazzi also provided Comey with the names of cyber criminals who had intercepted State Department emails and had offered them to countries hostile to the United States.

"Thanks to Ballestrazzi and the resources of INTERPOL," Comey's friend told the author of this book, "Jim felt his investigation was moving forward again. But he wasn't ready to share that information with the White House. Given the way the White House had behaved, Jim's turned down several requests from the president to go to the White House and talk things over.

"'As far as I'm concerned,' Jim told me, 'there's nothing to talk over.'"

CHAPTER
19

"My Worst Mistake as President"

When Valerie Jarrett entered the Oval Office, she found Barack Obama standing behind the Resolute desk, staring out the window at the Rose Garden.

"I appointed the son of a bitch. Doesn't he have to do what I say?" Obama said, according to Jarrett's recollection of the meeting, which she shared with a source who was interviewed for this book.

Obama didn't have to name the son of a bitch he was talking about. Jarrett knew he was referring to James Comey. Obama was furious with the FBI director for refusing a presidential request that he come to the White House to discuss the Hillary Clinton case.

"No," Jarrett said, "he doesn't have to do what you say any more than a judge you appoint has to."

"Giving Comey that job was probably my worst mistake as president," Obama said, according to Jarrett's recollection.

He paced back and forth, then flopped down on a sofa.

"I gave him the best job a cop could ever dream of," Obama said. "And what do I get in return? The son of a bitch is a registered Republican, and he knows damn well if he nails Hillary, he's going to throw the election to the Republicans."

Obama asked Jarrett what would happen if Comey recommended an indictment against Hillary. Would the White House get sufficient warning so that it would be prepared to handle the fallout? Jarrett assured him that Loretta Lynch would let him know the instant a referral came to her from the FBI.

"Most of the media are with us on this," Jarrett said. "*Politico* ran a long favorable piece saying that Hillary's case is different from cases where people were indicted for mishandling classified records, because in Hillary's case there was no intent."

The president made a face, as if to say he didn't set great store in that argument.

Jarrett noted that Comey's investigation had generated a full-blown public-relations war between the FBI and the White House. Shortly after Josh Earnest told the press corps that Hillary had done nothing to endanger national security, the FBI responded by rolling out the Romanian hacker Guccifer to tell TV reporters that he and others had breached Hillary's server, which of course was an assault on national security.

"Reporters wouldn't be allowed to interview Guccifer in jail unless Comey authorized it," Jarrett said. "We need to talk to Loretta. She's in charge of the Federal Bureau of Prisons, not Comey. She can prevent Guccifer from talking to the press."

Obama agreed, and Jarrett phoned Lynch, who promised to control the media's access to Guccifer while he was in federal prison.

"But," said Jarrett, recalling her conversation with the president as best as she could, "Loretta says that Comey can go around her in a number of ways. He can hold a suspect overseas, let him do taped TV interviews, and then release them here in the U.S. Loretta says, bottom line, she can't control Comey. He has a fanatical desire to bring Hillary down."

The discussion turned to the Clintons. Jarrett said Bill was talking trash about Obama, telling his friends in the press that the president of the United States could control the director of the FBI if he wanted to.

"Bill apparently thinks you're encouraging Comey," Jarrett said. "We should get word to him that we're on his side about this."

"Okay," Obama said, "but I don't want Bill to get the idea that I'm feeling goddam helpless at this point."

CHAPTER
20

The Blumenthal Ascendancy

I n many ways, Hillary trusted her three top aides—Huma Abe-din, Cheryl Mills, and Jake Sullivan—more than her own husband.

"Bill looks out for Bill first and foremost," she told a close friend. "And it's always been that way. But I know in my heart that Huma, Cheryl, and Jake will be loyal to the end. Especially Huma. Nothing will shake her loyalty. Huma would go to Sing Sing before she would rat me out to the FBI."

However, when Hillary found herself with her back to the wall—as she did now with the expanding FBI investigations into her emails and pay-to-play relationship with the Clinton

Foundation—the person she automatically turned to for help was Sidney Blumenthal.

They had known each other for more than thirty years, ever since Blumenthal was a young journalist covering the Clintons in Arkansas. He began crossing the line from journalist to propagandist during Bill Clinton's 1992 presidential campaign; Blumenthal defended Bill from accusations that he was a sexual predator. The friendship between Blumenthal and Hillary blossomed in 1997, when he went to work in the White House as the Clintons' chief communications adviser on the Monica Lewinsky scandal and coined the phrase "vast right-wing conspiracy" to discredit the Clintons' critics.

"Over the years" wrote *Politico*'s Glenn Thrush, "Blumenthal has corresponded more or less constantly with the Clintons, but especially Hillary, on a wide range of topics—not for nothing did he earn the nickname 'Grassy Knoll' for spinning dark conspiracy theories during his tenure in the White House during the Lewinsky scandal. Blumenthal's noir, wheels-within-wheels worldview meshed with the first lady's less-than-sunny view of the press and Republicans."

In a sworn deposition before a grand jury, Blumenthal testified that he had never fed defamatory information to reporters about Monica Lewinsky. But an old literary buddy, the late Christopher Hitchens, called Blumenthal a liar. Hitchens signed an affidavit claiming that Blumenthal had defamed Lewinsky as a "stalker" during a lunch with him. According to Hitchens, Blumenthal had perjured himself during his sworn testimony.

During the 2008 presidential primary campaign, Blumenthal spread scurrilous rumors about Barack Obama.

"Almost every day over the past six months," Professor Peter Dreier wrote in a May 2008 Huffington Post blog, "I have been the recipient of an email that attacks Obama's character, political views, electability, and real or manufactured associations. The original source of many of these hit pieces are virulent and sometimes extreme right-wing websites, bloggers, and publications. But they aren't being emailed out from some fringe right-wing group that somehow managed to get my email address. Instead, it is Sidney Blumenthal who, on a regular basis, methodically dispatches these email mudballs to an influential list of opinion shapers—including journalists, former Clinton administration officials, academics, policy entrepreneurs, and think tankers—in what is an obvious attempt to create an echo chamber that reverberates among talk shows, columnists, and Democratic Party funders and activists."

When Hillary later tried to hire Blumenthal as an adviser at the State Department, Rahm Emanuel, Obama's first chief of staff, vetoed the idea. The president didn't want to have anything to do with the reviled Blumenthal.

For a while, Blumenthal disappeared from the media's radar, but he was back on the screen when the State Department started releasing tranches of Hillary's emails. The emails revealed that Hillary had ignored Rahm Emanuel's orders and had secretly gone behind the White House's back to use Blumenthal as her own private intelligence-gathering service. In a flurry of emails,

Blumenthal had passed on gossip and advice to Hillary on a variety of foreign policy subjects—from Prime Minister Gordon Brown's chances of holding onto his job in Great Britain (he wrongly predicted that Brown would defeat David Cameron) to how the United States should deal with Libya.

A batch of 550 emails released in February 2016 contained a classic Blumenthal "Grassy Knoll" memo to Clinton titled "OBL photos." In this email, Blumenthal suggested that the administration use grisly photographs of Osama bin Laden's dead body to shore up Obama's image as a can-do president and influence the outcome of pending legislation in Congress.

"Having the whole Congress see the photos," Blumenthal wrote Clinton, "would have these likely impacts as well: The far–right-wing Tea Party Republicans would by [the photos'] mere presence admit to the President's status above them and to his effectiveness."

"Reading through the Blumenthal emails," wrote the *Washington Post*'s Fact Checker Glenn Kessler, "one sees that this is mostly gossip of dubious value."

The value of Blumenthal's advice was further tainted by his shameless conflicts of interest. While he was advising the secretary of state, he was also drawing salaries from the Clinton Foundation (which received a large chunk of its donations from foreign governments and businessmen), Media Matters (the Clinton's slime machine), and a company with business interests in Libya.

"When first asked about her correspondence with Blumenthal, Clinton insisted he was merely 'an old friend' who occasionally sent 'unsolicited' email," Jonah Goldberg wrote in *National*

Review. "That was a lie. It turns out that then-Secretary of State Clinton was in near-constant contact with Blumenthal, urging the head of her 'secret spy network' (ProPublica's term) to supply her with information and political advice, most about Libya.…

"But what does it say about Clinton that she just can't do without her pet?" Goldberg continued. "Part of the answer is that Blumenthal is a legendary sycophant. But the means of his sycophancy are more relevant. He serves as Clinton's enabler: a rumor-mongering Wormtongue whispering confirmation of the vast right-wing conspiracy that the Nixonian Clinton sees everywhere."

"Hillary doesn't give a shit what people say about Sid," a source close to the Clintons told the author of this book. "She loves him and knows he would kill for her."

In late May, after the FBI wrapped up its interviews with Huma and Cheryl and prepared to question Hillary, Blumenthal got in touch with Hillary and advocated a scorched earth policy against FBI Director James Comey. Hillary passed on some of Blumenthal's ideas to the top echelon in her Brooklyn campaign headquarters—chairman John Podesta, manager Robby Mook, and Huma Abedin—and to the dirty tricksters in her Slime Room, David Brock, and Hillary's truth-challenged spokesman Brian Fallon.

As usual, Blumenthal crossed the line of accepted opposition-research practices into the realm of dark conspiracy theories. He posited that anyone as devoutly Catholic as Comey must have skeletons in his closet of a sexual nature. Blumenthal rehashed widely debunked allegations that J. Edgar Hoover had been a cross-dresser, and suggested that Comey might have followed in Hoover's high-heel footsteps and was a cross-dresser, too.

He urged the campaign to put out these far-fetched claims, because he said that people were always ready to believe the worst about their enemies. Once the cross-dressing allegations hit the Internet, Blumenthal advised, they would go viral, and Comey would never be able to undo the damage to his reputation.

"Word about Blumenthal's dirty-tricks strategy percolated through the Brooklyn headquarters," said a source close to the campaign. "I was with a young lawyer from the campaign and two female volunteers at a bar near the headquarters, and we began talking about whether Sid's plan would work and prevent Hillary from being indicted.

"One of the girls asked me if I thought it was possible that Hillary could be indicted, and when I said the obvious—of course it was possible—she looked shocked and burst into tears. Until recently, this young woman and most of the others in the campaign thought that Hillary was in the clear. They told themselves they were off to the White House with the first woman president. But Sid's proposed plots were a wakeup call that things were going to get rough, and Hillary might not make it. And you could feel it in the atmosphere in Brooklyn—a sense of depression and dread."

PART 7

DONALD

VS.

HILLARY

Q. *Do the things that make a businessman great make a president great?*
A. *They help—but it's another step. You have to have a lot of different skills in addition to those of a businessman. You need a great communication skill, which a businessman does not need. You need a lot of heart; businessmen don't necessarily need heart.*

—Donald Trump, *Fortune* magazine, May 1, 2016

CHAPTER
21

Trump Force One

"I have friends who can have war with someone and then go back and be best friends. I can't be that way.... You have to remember who the loyal ones were and who were not, and if you don't you're a total schmuck. And if I have a chance to hurt these people who weren't loyal to me, I will. Call that vindictive. Call it what you will.... People who wouldn't talk to me three years ago now call up and want to kiss my ass. I tell my secretary, 'Rhona, call them back and say, "Mr. Trump told me to tell you, 'Fuck you!'" then hang up.'"

That was the rancorous forty-eight-year-old Donald Trump speaking to me for a *Vanity Fair* cover story that I wrote about his financial comeback and his new bride, Marla Maples, in the winter of 1994. By then, I had known Trump for almost fifteen years—ever since I was the editor in chief of the *New York Times* magazine and he invited me to Trump Tower with the hope of interesting me in assigning a story on the renovations he was making to his triplex apartment, which consisted of more than fifty rooms, including an eighty-foot-long living room with a waterfall.

The story never ran, but over the years Trump and I stayed in touch—on the phone and at his office on Fifth Avenue or his private club, Mar-a-Lago, in Palm Beach. In 2012, I wrote another cover story about him. Published by *Newsmax* magazine, it was titled "The Trump Effect" and it described his mounting influence in the Republican Party.

That magazine piece revealed a Trump whose combative temperament hadn't changed one iota. He still insulted people in a way that reminded you of a Don Rickles roast. And he was still in love with the first person singular. But one thing *had* changed: at sixty-six years of age, Trump's ambitions extended far beyond the world of New York real estate to Washington and the White House.

"I do nothing but fire people on television," he told me, "and yet millions across America respect my political opinions. I don't know if they like me personally, but I have political influence because people respect what I have to say and how I say it."

When Trump announced on June 16, 2015, that he was running for president, very few people took him seriously. The experts said he couldn't win the Republican nomination, and if by some wild set of circumstances he did, he'd be demolished by Hillary

Clinton, who was expected to sashay through the primaries and be crowned at the Democratic convention in Philadelphia.

But I had written four books about Hillary and I knew that her wooden inauthenticity and unlikeability would make her the perfect foil for the tell-it-like-it-is Trump. In fact, I felt that with Hillary as the Democrat nominee, Trump had a real chance to become president of the United States.

And so I met with Trump and told him that I wanted to spend some time with him on his campaign plane—the private Boeing 757-200 airliner that reporters dubbed Trump Force One. He didn't say yes and he didn't say no—a typical Trumpian negotiating ploy—and he remained noncommittal in several subsequent conversations. It wasn't until eleven months after my initial request that Rhona Graff, Trump's gal Friday, called and said, "If you can be at the Marine Air Terminal at LaGuardia nine o'clock tomorrow morning, you can fly with Donald to Indiana."

The *Washington Post* once described Trump's plane as a "gold-plated flying office and home," and that's what I expected to find when I entered the 757's spacious cabin. However, there was nothing garish about Trump Force One's cream-colored leather armchairs and sofas, inlaid mahogany tables, and conservatively dressed crew.

"This is Paul Allen's old plane," Trump told me, referring to the cofounder of Microsoft. "I gutted it and redid it. A nice way to travel, no?"

He sounded as though he was still amazed at how far he had traveled from his family's red brick home in the Jamaica Estates section of Queens. In fact, he turned to me more than once during the trip and said, "Can you believe it? I never expected to be here." He had vanquished fourteen of his original sixteen primary opponents, leaving only Senator Ted Cruz and Governor John Kasich standing between him and the Republican nomination.

At this stage of the race, any other candidate in Trump's post position would have been traveling with a staff of a dozen or more. But Trump had taken along just three people: his then campaign manager Corey Lewandowski, an adviser on social media, and an adviser on policy.

In most campaigns, you can feel the we-band-of-brothers relationship between the candidate and his advisers. That atmosphere was missing on Trump's plane. He sat alone in his Brioni blue suit and extra-long red tie throughout the entire trip, and when Lewandowski approached and addressed him, it was always with the respectful "Sir," never "Donald."

As the plane headed for Indianapolis, Trump took charge of the box that controlled the fifty-seven-inch flat-screen TV. He turned up the volume and began surfing channels, checking to see which Sunday news show was talking about him.

John Dickerson, the host of CBS News' *Face the Nation*, was interviewing Senator Lindsey Graham of South Carolina, who did not disguise his contempt for Trump.

"And there's been a lot of talk about Lucifer," Graham said. "I think Lucifer may be the only person Trump could beat in a general election."

Trump shouted over his shoulder to Lewandowski: "Write an email to CBS. 'Why don't you explain to your viewers that I beat [Graham] and drove him out of the race like a little boy.' Send it to Dickerson, and tell him it's really unfair to have a guest like that who is unchecked. Send it to John Dickerson from me."

Time after time, Trump reacted to the TV as if the people on the screen were actually present on the plane. If someone said something negative about him, he yelled at the screen and then barked out an order to Lewandowski: "Send an email!"

After a while, he returned to his chair, put on a pair of reading glasses, and began going through a stack of newspapers. As he read, he scrawled notes with a black Sharpie marker, signed them with an indecipherable Donald J. Trump, and clipped them out. They were punchy Trumpian missives to be snail-mailed or digitalized and emailed to people he wanted to thank, criticize, flatter, or degrade.

Most people assumed Trump winged it when he spoke in public. Actually, he prepared his lines as carefully as a trained stage actor. With his black Sharpie, he scribbled talking points on several pages of eight-by-eleven computer paper, which he carefully folded in half the long way and slipped into his inside jacket pocket, to be produced later when he made a speech.

He was an inveterate multi-tasker: while he wrote his speech notes, he chatted with me, gave instructions to his staff, ate a hamburger and fries, and talked to the TV. When Ted Cruz appeared on one of the news shows, Trump said, "I've beaten him eleven times in a row. I don't know why Cruz doesn't just come out and say I can't support Donald. I'd rather he doesn't support me."

Flipping to another channel, he watched Robert Gates plug his book, *Duty: Memoirs of a Secretary at War*, in which the former secretary of defense criticized president Obama's leadership in Afghanistan.

"You know," Trump said to me, "I have confidentiality agreements with everyone who works for me, and I think I'll do that in the White House so fucking guys like Gates can't write a book and trash everyone he worked with."

On the Fox News Channel, a reporter declared that Trump had a fifteen-point lead over Cruz in Indiana. But the news also included a Gallup poll showing that seven out of ten women had an unfavorable opinion of Trump. This set him off on a monologue about his relationship with women voters.

"You know, I'm going to do Megyn [Kelly] on Fox," he said. "It's a perfect opportunity to address the woman issue. The women will come around when they hear me discuss security, the border, and jobs. I've got sixteen million followers on Twitter, Facebook, and Instagram combined. The only thing Hillary's got going for her is she's a woman."

███

Eleven Secret Service agents accompanied Trump on the trip to Terre Haute, his first stop in Indiana, but the person who was closest to his side when he got off the plane was Keith Schiller, a former NYPD detective who has been Trump's personal bodyguard for the past seventeen years. The street-smart Schiller has gotten Trump out of a lot of scrapes, but his duties went beyond protection. He also carried a bottle of Purell hand sanitizer for the germophobic Trump, a can of hairspray, and a compact makeup to keep the candidate looking bronzed and healthy.

On the tarmac were more Secret Service agents plus a police escort that whisked Trump's motorcade into downtown Terre Haute. There, in a holding area in the historic Indiana Theatre, Trump greeted a score of local dignitaries and campaign workers, each of whom brought along a smart phone to have his or her photo taken with the candidate. Trump always assumed the same pose for the camera: eyes in a resolute squint, lower lip in a Churchillian pout, and right hand in a thumbs-up gesture.

The media reported that Trump appealed almost exclusively to uneducated lower-class white men, but as he took the stage in the Indiana Theatre, I took note of the crowd. There were as many women as men, and they did not look poor or badly dressed. A number of them had brought along their children and turned the event into a family outing.

They were so excited to see the TV celebrity-billionaire-candidate in the flesh that they stood during his entire fifty-five-minute speech, which Trump delivered with an occasional glance at his black Sharpie notes.

"Heidi Cruz says her husband was an immigrant," Trump told the crowd, referring to the wife of his opponent, Ted Cruz. "I don't want to cause any problems...."

You could hear the laughter starting to build.

"...and he's not going to win anyway...."

Now, the laughter was mixed with a rising wave of applause.

"He's walking in the beautiful halls of Congress afterward and meets his best friend, [Alabama Senator] Jeff Sessions who, by the way in case you didn't notice, endorsed me!"

Loud cheers and whistles.

"People hate that guy [Cruz]!"

The place went wild.

The crowd loved it even more when he took a shot at Hillary.

"Iraq is a crooked government," he said. "Hillary should run Iraq. That's where we should put her."

Mention of Hillary led him to free associate about women.

"Women want to see a strong country, a strong border, and strong jobs," he said, repeating what he had told me.

The women in the front row of the audience, many of whom were wearing Trump T-shirts, jumped up and down, their faces beet red from screaming at the top of their lungs.

At one point during the trip, Trump stopped at Shapiro's kosher-style delicatessen in Indianapolis to give the traveling press corps a chance to photograph him pressing the flesh with every-day Indianans. He ordered a Reuben sandwich and tossed the bread aside. He explained he was trying to cut down on carbs (although on another occasion, I saw him finish off a bucket of Kentucky Fried Chicken). He shooed the photographers away, because he didn't want to be caught like "disgusting" John Kasich shoveling food in his mouth.

As we got up from the table, Phillip Rucker of the *Washington Post* sidled up to me.

I knew of Rucker's reputation. During the 2012 presidential race, he covered Mitt Romney, and when Romney visited Poland's Tomb of the Unknown Soldier in Warsaw, Rucker interrupted the solemn ceremony and shouted out, "What about your gaffes!"

I didn't expect to be treated with any more civility than Romney.

"What are you doing here?" Rucker asked.

"I'm doing a book on the campaign and traveling with Trump," I replied.

The next day, Rucker's piece appeared in the *Washington Post* along with a concocted conspiracy theory: I had gone to Indiana, said Rucker, to feed Trump dirt about Hillary.

Rucker never checked with me before he wrote his fabricated story, and in point of fact, Trump and I didn't exchange ten words about Hillary during the entire two days I was with him.

CHAPTER
22

"Crooked Hillary"

everal weeks after the trip to Indiana, where Trump
drove Cruz and Kasich out of the race and cinched the
nomination, he called me. He wanted to vent about the
beating he was getting in the media.

"Can you believe what they're saying about me?" he said.
"The crooked media hammer me every day with nasty stories and
let Hillary get off without a word!"

He had a point.

For example, Martin Barron, the executive editor of the
Washington Post, denied that Amazon founder Jeff Bezos, who
owns the *Post*, tried to sway the paper's coverage of the campaign.
But Bob Woodward, the *Post*'s most famous reporter, admitted

that Bezos had indeed inserted himself into the paper's coverage
and urged the staff to "tell us everything about who the eventual
nominee will be in both parties." As a result, Woodward said, the
paper was unleashing an army of twenty reporters to dig up dirt
on Trump. Asked how many reporters the *Post* had assigned to
do a similar excavation of Hillary, Woodward hemmed and
hawed but couldn't come up with an answer.

Magazines and newspapers interviewed psychotherapists in
an effort to prove that Trump suffered from a pathological narcissistic personality disorder. They echoed Hillary's charge that
he was temperamentally unsuited to be president. The *New York
Times* criticized Trump for his alleged mistreatment of women
("Crossing the Line: How Donald Trump Behaved with Women
in Private"); his presumed political incompetence ("Donald
Trump's Campaign Stumbles as It Tries to Go Big"); his suppos-
edly misbegotten foreign policy ("In Donald Trump's Worldview, America Comes First, and Everybody Else Pays"); his
purported dodgy business dealings ("Testimony Calls Trump's
School Unscrupulous"); and his implied resemblance to Adolf
Hitler ("Rise of Donald Trump Tracks Growing Debate Over
Global Fascism").

"The *Times* accuses me of being a fascist on page one, but
buries the story of my sewing up the Republican nomination on
page A15," Trump told me. "The *Times* runs a story on my treatment of women, but all the girls it quotes as sources come out in
public voluntarily and defend me. The *Times* says Hillary has
eight hundred people on her staff, and I only have seventy. I do

more with less. Isn't that what the American people want in a leader?"

████

That Trump was the victim of blatant bias by the media was obvious to any fair observer. Even the *Times*' media reporter, Jim Rutenberg, admitted as much.

"If you're a working journalist," wrote Rutenberg, "and you believe that Donald J. Trump is a demagogue playing to the nation's worst racist and nationalistic tendencies, that he cozies up to anti-American dictators and that he would be dangerous with control of the United States nuclear codes, how the heck are you supposed to cover him?

"Because if you believe all of those things," Rutenberg continued, "you have to throw out the textbook American journalism has been using for the better part of the past half-century, if not longer, and approach it in a way you've never approached anything in your career."

And most reporters did throw out the journalism textbook.

"The shameful display of naked partisanship by the elite media is unlike anything seen in modern America," wrote Michael Goodwin, the *New York Post*'s Pulitzer Prize–winning columnist. "The largest broadcast networks—CBS, NBC and ABC—and major newspapers like *The New York Times* and *Washington Post* have jettisoned all pretense of fair play. Their fierce determination to keep Trump out of the Oval Office has no precedent."

Even liberal journalists interviewed by *The Hill*, a newspaper and website covering politics, agreed with Goodwin's alarming diagnosis of the ideological disease afflicting the media.

"Independent media watchers say that an emboldened press has found new and unorthodox ways to cover Trump that are at odds with past norms or how Hillary Clinton is covered," wrote *The Hill*'s Jonathan Easley. "And liberal writers Ezra Klein at *Vox* and Matt Taibbi of *Rolling Stone* took to their pages...to argue that many journalists have dropped any veneer of impartiality in covering Trump...[Ezra] Klein pointed to CNN fact-checking Trump on-screen and in real-time—something they have yet to do for Clinton. He noted that Buzzfeed is allowing reporters to describe Trump as a 'mendacious racist.'" And the Huffington Post even took to ending its stories on Trump with a disclaimer: "Donald Trump is a serial liar, rampant xenophobe, racist, misogynist, birther and bully who has repeatedly promised to ban all Muslims—1.6 million members of an entire religion—from entering the U.S." So much for fair and balanced reporting.

■■■■

Trump, however, had devised an ingenious way to ward off the attacks by his enemies in the mainstream media.

Between Twitter, Facebook, and Instagram, he had 16 million followers on social media. He used that vast audience to taunt his political opponents with malicious nicknames—"Low energy" Bush; "Little Marco"; "Lyin' Ted." On Saturday, April 16, 2016, during a rally in Watertown, New York, Trump gave Hillary a new moniker. Playing on the FBI investigation, Trump dubbed her "Crooked Hillary."

The next day, he tweeted the following 135 characters:

@realDonald Trump
Crooked Hillary Clinton is spending a fortune on ads against me. I am the one person she doesn't want to run against. Will be such fun!

That Sunday, George Stephanopoulos, the host of ABC's *This Week*, asked Hillary about her place in Trump's pantheon of nicknames

"That's the new nickname, Crooked Hillary," Stephanopoulos said. "Your response?"

"I don't respond to Donald Trump and his string of insults, uh, about me," Hillary replied. "I can take care of myself. I look forward to running against him if he turns out to be the Republican nominee if I am the Democratic nominee. What I'm concerned about is how he goes after everybody else. He goes after women. He goes after Muslims. He goes after immigrants. He goes after people with disabilities. He is hurting our unity at home."

As the campaign progressed, it became clear that Trump had adopted what might be called the Cold War doctrine of "massive retaliation." It had worked for him in the thirteen Republican primary debates; it had worked for him in hundreds of TV and radio interviews; and he was ready to make it work for him now in his response to Hillary.

"She's been crooked from the beginning," he said the next day during a rally in Buffalo, New York. "And to think, she has a shot at being our president? Crooked Hillary Clinton—we can't let that happen! You can't let that happen! And let me tell you, the only person that crooked Hillary Clinton does not want to run against is Donald Trump!"

From then on, Trump rarely missed an opportunity to mock "Crooked Hillary." The moniker became so popular among Republicans that Sean Spicer, the chief strategist and communications director of the Republican National Committee, adopted the nickname when he sent out a memo.

"Hillary Clinton's dishonesty has caught up with her again," Spicer wrote. "And with the Judicial Watch lawsuit and the FBI investigation still rolling full steam ahead, the worst of Hillary Clinton's woes over her secret email server may still be yet to come. It's going to be a long summer for Crooked Hillary."

At a Trump campaign stop in San Jose, the crowd started chanting "Lyin' Ted, Lyin' Ted," but Trump raised a hand to stop them.

"I want to save that now for Hillary—lying, lying Hillary," he told the crowd. "We don't say 'Lyin' Ted' anymore. We love Ted, we love him, right?...I'd love to pull it out and just use it on lying, crooked Hillary because she is a liar."

For a long time, Hillary seemed dazed and confused by Trump's insult-laden assaults, and Democrats were near panic over her seeming inability to mount an effective response. She was about to make history by becoming the first woman nominee of a major political party, and yet she couldn't shake Bernie Sanders or cope with Donald Trump, whose recent surge in the polls put the general election race in a dead heat.

The conventional wisdom among members of the chattering classes was that Hillary was a feeble candidate—maybe the weakest candidate the Democrats had put forward since 1984, when Ronald Regan carried 49 of the 50 states against Walter Mondale. And she and her much-vaunted campaign team didn't have a clue how to fix the problem.

But then Hillary sprung a surprise. Over a ten-day period, she worked with a team of speechwriters that included Jake Sullivan, her top policy aide, and Jon Favreau, a former speechwriter for Barack Obama, putting together an indignant riposte to Donald Trump. Another speechwriter, Megan Rooney, provided bits and pieces that reflected Hillary's natural biting sarcasm.

What followed was, for Hillary, a moment of at least temporary triumph.

CHAPTER

"Would Trump Be Worse?"

On June 2, 2016, in San Diego, Hillary delivered what the *Wall Street Journal* described as a "coruscating attack" on Trump. It was a vicious partisan polemic, full of stinging sarcasm, but it contained several charges against Trump that even many conservatives reluctantly conceded had some merit.

"Imagine Donald Trump sitting in the Situation Room, making life-or-death decisions on behalf of the United States," Hillary said in her speech. "Imagine if he had not just his Twitter account at his disposal when he's angry, but America's entire arsenal."

This was the ruthless and uncompromising Hillary that the liberal establishment had been hoping and praying for, and it excited them to madness.

"Hillary Clinton's blistering new assault on Donald J. Trump," crowed the *New York Times*, "has mollified many Democrats alarmed about the closer-than-expected presidential race.... Mixing stark warnings that Mr. Trump would imperil America's security with caustic personal critiques—'I'll leave it to the psychiatrists to explain his affection for tyrants'—Mrs. Clinton offered the first indication that she is willing to confront her unconventional opponent in the fashion many in her party believe his candidacy demands."

But the most remarkable thing about Hillary's speech was not that it allayed the fears of Democrats, but that it echoed many of the fears of conservatives, who were put off by Trump's insults and vulgarity, his lack of discipline, his unfamiliarity with economic and foreign policy issues, his attacks on fellow Republicans, and his dismissal of conservative principles.

"Mrs. Clinton has identified Mr. Trump's greatest liability, which is the Commander-in-Chief test," editorialized the *Wall Street Journal*, which spoke for the Republican establishment.

Columnist Peggy Noonan agreed that Trump had to clean up his act.

"GOP elites and intellectual cadres may be clueless about America right now," she wrote, "but they have an informed and appropriately elevated sense of the demands of the presidency. They fear Mr. Trump's temperament and depth do not meet its requirements.... The Beltway intelligentsia...claim that they'd support him but they have to be able to sleep at night."

One of the things that really pissed off conservatives was Trump's gratuitous attack on Susana Martinez, the popular two-term Republican governor of New Mexico.

"She's got to do a better job," Trump declared. "She's not doing the job."

Baffled conservatives couldn't understand why Trump, who by now was beginning to trail miserably in the polls with women and Hispanics, would pick on a Latina in a swing state who also happened to be the chairman of the Republican Governors Association.

Trump came up with an excuse that alternated between juvenile whining and defiant bombast.

"She was not nice," he said. "And I was fine—just a little bit of a jab. But she wasn't nice, and you think I'm going to change? I'm not changing, including with her."

"This politics of pique is more likely to achieve the opposite," the editors of the *Wall Street Journal* lectured Trump. "Mr. Trump's challenge, if he wants to win in November, includes persuading millions of Republicans who believe he's too crude and thuggish to build a political majority."

But what really got conservative nerves jangling was Trump's attack on U.S. District Judge Gonzalo Curiel, who was presiding over civil fraud lawsuits against Trump University. Trump said that Curiel had "an absolute conflict" because the judge, who was born in Indiana, was "a Mexican."

Practically the entire Republican establishment jumped down Trump's throat.

"Look," said House Speaker Paul Ryan, "the comment about the judge, just was out of left field for my mind. It's reasoning I don't relate to, I completely disagree with the thinking behind that. So he clearly says and does things I don't agree with and I've had to speak up on time to time when that has occurred and I'll continue to do that if that's necessary—I hope it's not."

Charles Krauthammer, the Pulitzer Prize–winning columnist and Fox News Channel analyst, was unsparing in his criticism of Trump.

"There are two disturbing elements in this," Krauthammer wrote. "The first has to do with ethnicity, the other has to do with respect for the constitutional structure. About ethnicity: You call a guy a Mexican who's an American citizen—born here, raised here—because of Mexican heritage. Imagine if he were to say, 'he's biased against me because he's a Jew or because he's black.' You can't do that in this country.

"The larger issue, apart from that, is a presidential candidate ranting against a sitting judge because of a private case, and the implication that there will be retaliation," Krauthammer continued. "We have had a quarter of a millennium [in the United States] where the executive has respected the independence of the judiciary—criticizing is one thing, but this idea of menacing it [is something else]."

A devil's advocate case could be made for Trump that he was only aping the identity politics of the Left. It was Supreme Court Justice Sonia Sotomayor, after all, who had said in a speech in 2001, when she was a federal judge, that "I hope that a wise Latina woman with the richness of her experiences would more often than not reach a better conclusion than a white male who hasn't lived that life."

And it was true that Judge Curiel belonged to a group called La Raza Lawyers, (*la raza* meaning "the race"), which is dedicated to promoting "the interests of the Latino communities" in California. Trump asserted that meant Judge Curiel would be biased against him because of Trump's strong stand on border security.

Trump attempted to clarify his position by stating, "It is unfortunate that my comments have been misconstrued as a categorical attack against people of Mexican heritage. I am friends with and employ thousands of people of Mexican and Hispanic descent. The American justice system relies on fair and impartial judges. All judges should be held to that standard. I do not feel that one's heritage makes them incapable of being impartial, but, based on the rulings that I have received in the Trump University civil case, I feel justified in questioning whether I am receiving a fair trial."

But few Republicans were willing to step forward to defend him. In fact, not just House Speaker Paul Ryan, but senior Republican figures like Newt Gingrich, Senate Majority Leader Mitch McConnell, and Senator Bob Corker, who chairs the Senate Foreign Relations Committee, made a point of distancing themselves from Trump. Even some of Trump's closest allies wondered why he had been so self-destructive with his controversial comments when he should have been concentrating his attention on the State Department inspector general's scathing report on Hillary Clinton's misuse of her email system.

One Republican statesman who had spent time with Trump wondered whether the candidate really wanted to be president.

"He does and says things," the statesman told me, "that can only be described as suicidal."

But the unlikely candidate, who talked like an old-style New York taxi driver, was still giving Hillary a run for her money. As Trump had said as early as 1988 in an interview with Oprah Winfrey, if he ran for president, he wouldn't "go in to lose."

████

And there was still a very good chance that Trump could win, despite the fears of the Republican establishment. In fact, the spectacle of conservatives piling on Trump reminded me of how the Republican establishment had treated Ronald Reagan in 1980. Craig Shirley, the author of several well-received books about Reagan, including *Rendezvous with Destiny: Ronald Reagan and the Campaign that Changed America*, discussed the parallels between Trump and Reagan when he appeared on *Morning Joe* in September 2015.

"In the '60s and '70s [Reagan] was often derided by the Eastern elites, by academia, by the establishment of the Republican party," said Shirley. "He was considered the George Wallace of the Republican party, a grade B actor with premature orange hair.

"In 1980," Shirley added, "as he started to break loose and head towards the nomination, the party elders in a panic, you know, ring the fire alarm, break the glass and go see Gerald Ford. Dick Cheney went to see him. Henry Kissinger tried to go see him to get Ford to get back in the race just to stop Ronald Reagan from the nomination."

The Dump Reagan movement fizzled, just as the Republicans' #NeverTrump movement was destined to flop. And the reasons for that were not hard to find.

First, once Trump had cleared the primary field, there were no credible alternatives—certainly not David French, the writer and Iraq war veteran who was briefly promoted as an independent conservative candidate by William Kristol, founder and editor of the *Weekly Standard*. Nobody outside a coterie of Manhattan intellectuals knew anything about French, and as soon as his name surfaced he showed good common sense and took himself out of the running.

Second—and most obvious—the Republican rank and file knew that every vote *against* Trump was a vote for Hillary; every *non-vote* by a stay-at-home registered Republican was a vote for Hillary; every vote for an *independent* conservative was a vote for Hillary.

So, for Republicans, Independents, "Reagan Democrats," and, if the polls were to be believed, even some Bernie Sanders Democrats, it all came down to a choice: Who did you want in the White House for the next four years—Donald Trump or Hillary Clinton? If you wanted change from the status quo, Trump was the hands-down winner. He was the consummate non-professional politician against the aging ideologue Hillary, who had been in politics for decades. Likewise, if you favored free-market capitalism, a smaller government, and more individual freedom, that choice was easy to make: Trump. Finally, if you simply didn't want to endure a Hillary Clinton presidency, the choice was simple: Trump.

While chattering class conservatives and establishment Republicans worried about a Trump presidency, average conservatives, even those who hadn't supported him in the primaries, were flocking to Trump's banner. They seemed to have a simple and obvious checklist. A Hillary Clinton presidency would mean:

- More taxpayer-financed "free stuff" for favored Democratic groups
- More national debt
- More business regulations
- More government-directed crony capitalism
- More layoffs
- More unconstitutional executive orders
- More politics of envy
- More illegal immigrants
- More Islamist terrorism
- More Clinton scandals
- More favors for big-bucks contributors
- More gridlock in Washington
- More division between blacks and whites
- More criticism of the police and more crime and disorder
- More Obamacare and higher premiums
- More downsizing of the armed forces
- More late-term abortions
- More out-of-wedlock children supported by welfare

- More gun control
- More federal control of public schools
- More "multi-gender" bathrooms
- More liberal Supreme Court justices
- More political correctness
- More assaults on free speech on college campuses
- More chaos in the Middle East
- More humiliation from China, Russia, and Iran
- More, in other words, of the last eight years under President Obama

Most conservatives—outside the beltway and outside intellectual salons at least—seemed to gladly echo the words of Pulitzer Prize–winning columnist Michael Goodwin: "Would Trump be worse?"

PART 8

THE CLINTONS

There's little doubt that today, what some in the Clinton orbit call the "invisible hand of Chelsea" shapes almost every significant decision her parents make.

—Kenney P. Vogel, *Politico*

CHAPTER
24

Hillary's "Valerie Jarrett"

Huma Abedin came down the stairs in Chappaqua, rubbing her puffy eyes and looking a bit disheveled.

"Did you get your power nap?" Hillary asked.

She placed both hands on Huma's neck and began massaging her shoulders.

"Huma smiled, but looked embarrassed," recalled one of Hillary's oldest friends, who had been invited along with a group of women to spend the afternoon with Hillary, and who spoke on the condition of anonymity because the Chappaqua get-together was private.* "Huma's tough, but there are times when

---

* The source was interviewed eighteen times.

she can look like a shy little girl, especially when Hillary displays an interest in her in front of other people."

Huma went off to a corner of the room to check on Hillary's emails, and one of the women handed Hillary a glass of Chardonnay. After a sip, Hillary recounted a conversation she had had with her lawyer, David Kendall, about the enemies who were closing in on her from all sides.

Trey Gowdy's Benghazi committee was about to release its long-anticipated report about Hillary's responsibility as secretary of state for the deaths of Ambassador Christopher Stevens and three other Americans.

"They're going to savage me," Hillary said.

Indeed, the committee's Republican majority viewed Hillary's failure to provide the Benghazi consulate with adequate security as an unpardonable dereliction of duty. The Republicans were equally outraged that Hillary had lied to the families of the dead Americans, telling them that the attack on the consulate was a spontaneous response to an anti-Islamic video, when in fact she had emailed Chelsea on the night of the deadly assault that it was a well-planned, al-Qaeda–sponsored attack.

On another front, U.S. District Court Judge Emmet G. Sullivan had granted Judicial Watch the right in its FOIA case to take testimony from Huma, Cheryl Mills, and Bryan Pagliano, the IT specialist who had been granted immunity from criminal prosecution by the Justice Department in return for testimony regarding Hillary's use of her private email server. Pagliano's immunity did not cover civil litigation such as the Judicial Watch case, and Hillary worried he might offer damaging testimony. Worse yet, Judge

Sullivan had ruled that Hillary herself might have to appear in court to answer questions under oath.

Then, of course, there was Hillary's nemesis, FBI Director James Comey.

"That asshole has been after me forever," Hillary said, according to the friend who was interviewed for this book. "Well, let him bring it on!" she added, pumping her fist in the air in a gesture of defiance.

To top it all off, Bernie Sanders had vowed to take the fight for a socialist "revolution" all the way to the Democratic National Convention in Philadelphia in late July.

"Bernie has shit all over my nomination," Hillary said. "That weasel tries to spoil everything."

Sanders had gotten under Hillary's skin by challenging her sense of entitlement—that she was "owed" her party's nomination—and when she called him a "weasel," she raised her arm as if to strike him, and half the wine in her glass went flying through the air.

"Good thing it wasn't Cabernet," she said.

While lunch was served, someone asked Hillary about Bill.

"I have no fucking idea where he is," she said. "Probably with some..."

She let the sentence hang in the air.

She went on to say that Bill was raising money for her campaign, but that she rarely saw him. He ran a completely separate operation from hers, wrote his own speeches, and arranged his own transportation. Her staff in Brooklyn had no idea where he was going next and what he was going to say. Hillary had long ago learned to live with Bill's idiosyncrasies (for want of a better word), but she was worried about recent signs that he was losing it.

"He blew up at the Black Lives Matter people," she complained, "and the whole episode was caught on video. That wasn't very fucking helpful. Then he got into an argument in front of the TV cameras with a Bernie supporter over his welfare program when he was president. Not fucking helpful!"

In a fit of pique, she grabbed a handful of her hair and in an odd mannerism, which her women friends had seen before, she yanked at the hair so hard it looked as though she was trying to pull it out.

"Hillary don't!" one of the women said.

Huma, who was sitting across the room, started to giggle. She caught Hillary's eye, and Hillary stopped pulling on her hair.

"Huma's seen this hair-pulling routine a hundred times, and she knows the best way to handle it is to make light of it," her friend recalled.

Hillary got up and said to Huma, "Okay, okay, let's take a quick walk to get the blood flowing before we get back to work."

"She and Huma walked out of the room together," said her friend, "and I thought at that moment, no wonder Chelsea's jealous and suspicious of her mother's relationship with Huma."

———

Chelsea Clinton was respectful of Huma when her mother was around, but she treated Huma with undisguised contempt when Hillary wasn't present. In fact, Chelsea seemed happiest when her mother chewed out Huma for doing something that displeased her. Hillary was aware of Chelsea's feelings, and she dismissed the whole thing as a case of natural sibling rivalry.

But the highly charged emotional triangle that existed among Hillary, Huma, and Chelsea was more complicated than that.

"Unlike Hillary's relationship with Huma, her relationship with Chelsea is remote and somewhat cold," said one of Hillary's friends. "Chelsea is not a warm person. I've never seen them embrace or kiss on the cheek or show any sign of affection, except when they're in public and putting on a show."

Like her rageaholic parents, Chelsea had a volcanic temper. She was both feared and loathed in Hillary's Brooklyn campaign headquarters. She interrupted meetings, made outrageous demands, and acted as though her mother had given her carte blanche to order people around. Several talented campaign workers quit because of Chelsea, and some of them joined the Bernie Sanders campaign.

Chelsea had a high opinion of her political judgment, and considered herself to be her mother's "Valerie Jarrett"—the one person Hillary listened to before she made any decision. She saw herself as the inheritor of her father's raw political talent, and was proud of her speaking skills in front of large audiences.

But she flopped on her first solo appearance on the 2016 stump. She viciously ripped into Bernie Sanders's single-payer healthcare proposal, shattering her image as the beloved and politically bulletproof first daughter. That prompted many Democrats, including David Axelrod, to recommend that Chelsea be restrained.

When Brian Fallon, the campaign spokesman, was asked by a reporter if Chelsea would continue to attack Sanders, and whether she was suited for such a role, he praised Chelsea as a "very spirited and fierce advocate" for Hillary, but he acknowledged that the campaign intended to rein her in.

That might have been wishful thinking. Now that her name was on the door of her family's multi-billion-dollar philanthropy—it was called the Bill, Hillary and Chelsea Clinton Foundation—she was more high-handed than ever. She didn't hesitate to second-guess Donna Shalala, the president of the foundation, and this often precipitated stormy family jousts with her parents.

More often than not, Chelsea took her mother's side against her father. Bill irritated Hillary with his constant lecturing on how she should do this or that—conduct her campaign, treat her staff, raise money, and deal with media. She preferred to have conversations with Bill on the phone so that she could hang up on him whenever he drove her crazy.

Most of all, Hillary hated to hear Bill opine on the FBI investigation and the chance that she might be indicted.

"Hillary gets very down when Bill introduces any negativity in their conversation," said a close family friend. "He can take a torrent of bad news and put it in his back pocket, but she finds it absolutely scary. Her face sags, her eyes shine, and she looks twenty years older. When a wave of depression sweeps over her, she has a hard time recovering, and if she has an important appearance or interview coming up, she often prefers to cancel it.

"Chelsea gets very annoyed with her father and has loudly told him to back off," the friend continued. "I've seen her point a finger right in his face. He literally bites his tongue. He's afraid of Chelsea's temper, and he's worried she'll yell at him in public the way she does when they're behind closed doors. She can be verbally abusive, and it really hurts his feelings. He's tough as nails when it comes to strangers, but not with his own daughter."

Each of the Clintons had a separate agenda, which caused constant familial conflict. For instance, Bill didn't want to live in the White House as first gentleman and relinquish his princely post-presidential lifestyle. His ambivalence about Hillary's campaign drove her crazy, because it threatened her lifetime dream of becoming the first woman president of the United States.

"Where Bill is reluctant to share the presidential arena with Hillary, Chelsea desperately wants her mother to win, because she sees herself, not her father, as becoming the co-president," said a longtime Clinton family confidant. "Bill won't be around the Oval Office much, but Chelsea will be right there at her mother's elbow. People talk about Chelsea becoming her mother's White House hostess, a kind of substitute first lady, but that's BS. As Chelsea sees it, she'll become her mother's chief political adviser.

"Having her mother in the White House will launch Chelsea's career like nothing else. It will bring her millions of dollars in speaking fees and book contracts. It will give her a platform on which to run for public office. And it will pave the way for her to become way more famous than just being an *ex*–first daughter."

It was the old Clinton story: everything they did was aimed at increasing their power, wealth, rank, and honor, and let the devil—and the country—take the hindmost.

CHAPTER

Fit to Lead?

The greatest fear among senior members of Hillary's staff was that if the "Comey primary" (shorthand for the FBI email investigation) didn't get her, her health would.

But no one in her campaign dared discuss the question of whether Hillary was medically fit to be commander in chief. Speaking about her health was the ultimate taboo.

Conveniently (at least for Hillary), the liberal mainstream media cooperated and chose to ignore the topic—even when a photo of Hillary, taken in February 2016, surfaced during the campaign showing her being assisted by two men as she stumbled up a short flight of stairs.

On the other hand, when Donald Trump, his surrogates, or conservative commentators like Sean Hannity raised the subject of Hillary's health, they were vilified and accused of trafficking in unsubstantiated rumors. Journalists were treated even worse; those who dared explore Hillary's health issues were accused of being dishonest, dishonorable, and discredited.

As a result, the public was left in the dark about Hillary's fitness to lead.

For years, Hillary had kept her medical history secret out of fear that, if it became public, it would knock her out of contention for the White House. But in December 2012, she suffered a medical emergency that couldn't be hidden from the public. Just before she was scheduled to testify on Benghazi in front of the Senate Foreign Relations Committee, she fainted in her seventh-floor office at the State Department.

It wasn't the first time that had happened. She had a fainting spell in 2005 during an appearance before a women's group in Buffalo, and another fainting spell in 2009 while boarding her plane in Yemen, where she fell and fractured an elbow.

In this latest incident at Foggy Bottom, she hit her head and suffered a concussion. She was treated at the State Department's infirmary and sent home to Whitehaven to recover.

When Bill appeared on the scene, however, he demanded that she be flown immediately to the New York-Presbyterian Hospital in Manhattan. There, doctors discovered that Hillary had a right transverse venous thrombosis, or blood clot, between her brain and skull. She had developed the clot in one of the veins that drains blood from the brain to the heart.

On further examination, it turned out that Hillary had an intrinsic tendency to form clots and faint. Several years earlier, she had developed a clot in her leg and was put on anticoagulant therapy by her doctor. However, she had stopped taking her anti-coagulant medication, which might have explained the most recent thrombotic event.

According to a source close to Hillary, a thorough examination revealed that Hillary's tendency to form clots was just one of her medical problems. She also suffered from a thyroid condition, which was common among women of her age, and had an undiagnosed heart problem, which probably contributed to the cause of her fainting spells. A cardiac stress test indicated that her heart rhythm and heart valves were not normal.

At the time, I tried to contact the Clintons' cardiologist, Dr. Allan Schwartz. He refused to take my call. However, I learned through other channels that Hillary's doctors considered performing valve-replacement surgery. They ultimately decided against it for reasons that were never made clear, although some sources speculated that Hillary did not want to risk the negative political fallout from stories about such a serious operation.

After her concussion, Hillary had trouble with her vision and had to wear corrective Fresnel prism lenses, which gave rise to questions about the long-term seriousness of her condition. Her chief flack, Philippe Reines ("Lyin' Phil" in Donald Trump argot), tried to make light of it; he claimed that she had recovered in a snap. But Bill Clinton revealed the true nature of her condition when he said that it had taken Hillary "six months of very serious work" to recuperate from her concussion.

A year after her doctors discovered the blood clot on Hillary's brain, she was still on a blood thinner. And there were reports that she might be suffering from post-concussion syndrome, a disorder that can have a severe effect on a person's cognitive abilities.

━━━━

The presidency is the most stressful job in the world, and the physical condition of those who aspire to the office is of vital importance. In my book, *Unlikeable: The Problem with Hillary,* I devoted five pages to an exploration of Hillary's health. As far as I could tell, I was the first journalist to explore this critically important subject in depth.

In July 2015—three months after she announced her intention to seek the presidency—Hillary's longtime personal physician, Dr. Lisa Bardack, released a two-page letter that was aimed at giving Hillary a clean bill of health.

"She does not smoke and drinks alcohol occasionally," Dr. Bardack wrote. "She does not use illicit drugs or tobacco products. She eats a diet rich in lean protein, vegetables and fruits. She exercises regularly, including yoga, swimming, walking and weight training."

According to Dr. Bardack, Hillary had recovered completely from the concussion and the blood clot in her brain.

But there were several problems with Dr. Bardack's letter. According to interviews that I conducted with several of Hillary's close friends, she drank wine or beer every day, had no interest in yoga, did not use a personal trainer to do weight training, and got most of her exercise by strolling around Chappaqua or walking in Rock Creek Park near her home in Washington.

In fact, Hillary still suffered from many of the troubling symptoms that I wrote about in *Unlikeable*: blinding headaches, exhaustion, insomnia, and a tremor in her hands.

As a precaution against the spectacle of her fainting again—this time in public, which could easily doom her candidacy—Bill insisted that Hillary travel with a personal physician. At first, she resisted his advice. But he enlisted the support of the Secret Service and his friend Dr. Dean Ornish, who had put Bill on a low-sugar, plant-heavy, low-fat diet. Together with Dr. Ornish, Bill found a suitable physician to travel with Hillary and keep her under constant medical observation.

Since then, there have been several troubling incidents, all of which have been kept from the news media. For example, after her eleven-hour testimony before the Trey Gowdy Benghazi committee, Hillary swooned as she walked to her waiting car. She had to be carried by her aides and conveyed into the back seat.

Tension headaches continued to plague her and often made it hard for her to maintain her grueling campaign schedule, or to concentrate on a subject. In one of the emails released by the State Department, Huma confessed that Hillary was easily "confused." Huma frequently ordered campaign aides to alter Hillary's schedule at the last moment so the candidate could catch her breath and take time out for naps.

That might have explained why Hillary was often as much as two hours late for campaign appearances—and why she was late in returning from a "bathroom break" during a televised Democrat debate in December.

"She no longer has the stamina for eighteen-hour campaign days that she was once capable of doing," said a source close to Hillary.

It went without saying that the presidency was a twenty-four-hour-a-day job.

————

In April 2016, Hillary had a coughing fit while being interviewed on *The Breakfast Club*, one of New York's top-rated radio shows among African Americans.

"Allergy season," she gasped. "My voice is failing here."

Within minutes, my email inbox was filled with questions: Did Hillary's frequent bouts of coughing prove she was hiding a serious health problem? And what about her renewed use of those thick eyeglasses to correct double vision?

Bill's worst fear, according to my sources, was that Hillary would faint at a critical moment in the campaign and reveal the truth about her physical condition. If people knew the full extent of her medical problems, they might question her fitness for the job of commander in chief. Everything had to be done to hide the truth.

To get to the bottom of this matter, I turned to one of Hillary's oldest friends who has known her for almost fifty years. This woman frequently speaks with Hillary on the phone, and visits her at her homes in Chappaqua and Washington, D.C. Hillary trusts her and confides in her.*

"Bill told me that he is very worried about Hillary's health," this woman said. "She is not steady on her feet, frequently gets dizzy, and often needs help to climb stairs and even to stand for long periods. Bill is concerned and wants her to have tests run. But she refuses, saying she doesn't need it and fears any tests she had done might be leaked to the press or get posted on the Internet.

"I've noticed that she has her legs elevated most of the time when she is out of public view," she continued. "Huma often brings her a cool water-soaked towel, which she applies to her forehead and her neck. She has terrible headaches that make her sag like she is going to fall over.

"Huma always kneels down, whispers to her, rubs her shoulders, and comforts her. Huma often seems genuinely alarmed at her condition, and looks agonized as well.

"Hillary also has a masseuse on call to work on her legs, which give her almost constant pain. It reminds me of what I read about Jack Kennedy's constant back problems and how they were always hidden from the public.

---

* Some readers might wonder why a F.O.H.—Friend of Hillary—would talk to an author who is known for his critical books about Hillary. There are several explanations. First, this friend of Hillary's has been a source for several of my books, and I have always protected her anonymity. Second, in describing Hillary's health, this woman exhibited a deep concern for her old friend. Third, like all sources who speak anonymously about their powerful friends, she is aware of her own importance as a witness to events. And fourth and perhaps most important, friends of powerful people often harbor a natural human ambivalence about someone who is "above them," and by talking to an author they feel they are evening things out.

"Unfortunately for Hillary, a lot of the things that are written about her health on social media sites are purely speculative. But she and Bill and all the members of their inner circles are growing more and more alarmed that her health problems are going to be a huge issue in the campaign. Trump clearly revels in bringing it up and realizes he gets a great deal of press from it.

"Hillary has said that she should get sympathy from a lot of voters over the fact that she is suffering aches and pains like most everyone else her age. She looks to me to be in absolute agony a lot of the time, particularly when she has been on her campaign trail for long periods of time.

"Her campaign people are well aware of her problems and are doing everything possible to make her schedule as easy as possible, but it's hard to run for president and not work hard and spend a lot of time on your feet and constantly get photographed.

"She believes that for the most part the press has been very considerate, withholding the worst pictures of her, particularly the ones of her looking like she is in agony, or worse, simply confused. I'm convinced that if it was up to Bill he would shut down the campaign and end it. But Hillary would rather die than do that. I think it is fair to say that the biggest issue behind the scenes with the campaign is Hillary's health."

CHAPTER
26

A Tissue of Lies

"**I** don't want any risk of the personal being accessible."

That's what Hillary emailed Huma Abedin when she was secretary of state. And that email—like a trace of DNA in a murder investigation—proved beyond a shadow of a doubt that Hillary was guilty as sin.

Hillary *intentionally* took steps to violate federal recordkeeping laws.

"Hillary Clinton did not want her emails subjected to the Freedom of Information Act or subpoenas from Congress, and that's why she set up a home-brew server," Carl Bernstein of Watergate fame told CNN. "I think we all know that. People round her will tell you that in private if you really get them behind closed doors."

Bob Woodward of the Woodward and Bernstein Watergate scoops went even further.

"Follow the trail here," Woodward said on MSNBC's *Morning Joe*. "There are all these emails.... You've got a massive amount of data—in a way, reminds me of the Nixon tapes: thousands of hours of secretly recorded conversations that Nixon thought were exclusively his."

On May 25, 2016, the State Department's inspector general—the ombudsman charged with keeping the department on the straight and narrow—issued a scathing report on Hillary's exclusive use of a private email server.

The seventy-nine-page report demolished her tissue of lies. Hillary had repeatedly assured reporters, "I'm more than ready to talk to anybody anytime" about her emails, but the report revealed that Hillary and most of her top aides—Huma, Cheryl, and nearly two dozen others—defiantly stonewalled the IG by refusing to submit to requests for interviews.

Hillary's claim that the State Department had "allowed" such a private email arrangement was exposed by the IG report as patently untrue. On the contrary, said the IG, Hillary had failed to seek permission to use a private email system, and if she had sought such permission, it would have been refused.

What's more, she failed to adhere to the department's rules—and federal laws—that governed the proper handling of records.

"Secretary Clinton," the report said, "should have surrendered all emails dealing with department business before leaving government service and, because she did not do so, she did not comply with the department's policies that were implemented in accordance with the Federal Records Act."

More than 60 percent of Americans already believed that Hillary was untrustworthy and a congenital liar; the IG's report confirmed that suspicion. In an effort to debunk the IG's report, Hillary's vast communications apparatus, a.k.a. the Clinton Slime Room, went on the offensive. In an interview with Univision's Maria Elena Salinas, Hillary refused to admit any fault in the handling of her emails. She claimed that everything that she had done other secretaries of state had also done.

Her claims of innocence, however, did not stack up against the truth. For example:

What Hillary Said: "None of the emails contained classified data."

The Truth: Some 2,200 of her emails contained classified documents, and more than twenty of those were SAPs, Special Access Programs, which meant they were beyond top-secret. The sensitive nature of those documents would have been obvious to a college freshman, and certainly to anyone who, like Hillary, had been given a two-hour tutorial by two FBI agents on how to identify information affecting national security. To take just five examples, Hillary's emails included classified information about 1) Iran's nuclear facilities; 2) North Korea's nuclear program; 3) a meeting involving the Taliban; 4) a memo from then CIA Director David Petraeus's chief of staff; and 5) information regarding pending CIA drone strikes in Pakistan.

What Hillary Said: "None of the emails were marked classified."

The Truth: That was irrelevant. As a high-ranking officer of the government, she had an obligation under the law to know how to recognize state secrets and care for them. "Clinton knowingly diverted all of her governmental emails from secure government servers to her own non-secure server in her New York residence," wrote Judge Andrew P. Napolitano, a Fox News contributor. "Among the 60,000 emails she diverted were 2,200 that contained state secrets. Because the essence of espionage is the removal of secrets to non-secure venues, the crime is complete upon removal.... You don't have to prove intent when you're talking about espionage; you can prove it by gross negligence [and] there's ample evidence of gross negligence."

What Hillary Said: The private unsecure email system was never hacked.

The Truth: The server was temporarily unplugged in 2015 because a Clinton aide discovered that "someone was trying to hack us." That information was not reported to the State Department, as required by regulations and the law. The hacker Guccifer testified that he and others had hacked into Hillary's email server. The server "was directly connected to the Internet in ways that made it more vulnerable to hackers," reported the Associated Press's Deb Riechmann.

What Hillary Said: "Just like previous secretaries of state, I used a personal email. Many people did it. It was not at all unprecedented."

The Truth: No previous secretary of state had a home-brew server. No previous secretary of state used a private email address exclusively. Colin Powell used a private email address *before* the current State Department rules forbidding that went into effect.

What Hillary Said: "I have turned over all my emails.... I have been incredibly open about doing that."

The Truth: She didn't turn over all her emails, and she certainly didn't turn them over voluntarily. According to the *Washington Post*'s Roz Helderman and Tom Hamburger, Hillary turned over her emails "only after the State Department requested them as it prepared responses for the Republican-led House committee investigation into the 2012 attack on U.S. diplomats in Benghazi, Libya." She deleted about half of her sixty thousand emails, claiming they were "personal," but no one was allowed to check on her claim because she wiped her server clean in an effort to leave no traces. The batch of emails she reluctantly turned over to the State Department was far from complete; thousands more, including emails about Benghazi and the Clinton Foundation, eventually turned up after her initial dump.

Hillary's obsession with secrecy was nothing new.

Over a period of four decades—from Whitewater to her email scandal to her pay-to-play link with the Clinton Foundation—Hillary lied, dissembled, and put up a false front.

Shortly after she and Bill moved into the White House in January 1993, Hillary threw a fit when stories began to appear that she had hurled a lamp at her husband and called him a "stupid motherfucker." Many family newspapers found it impossible to print her foul-mouthed eruptions, such as the time she burst into a room looking for Bill and shouted at a Secret Service officer, "Where's the miserable cocksucker?"

"She blamed these press leaks on the Secret Service officers who were stationed in the private residence, and she had them banished from the family quarters, where they had stood vigil since Ronald Reagan's presidency," I reported in my 2005 book *The Truth about Hillary: What She Knew, When She Knew It, and How Far She'll Go to Become President.* "The officers were moved down one level, where they could no longer witness the Clintons' *Jerry Springer*-style free-for-alls."

Hillary's mistrustful nature became more apparent once she became an equal partner in Bill's presidency.

"Breaking decades of tradition," Robert Pear reported in the *New York Times* two days after Bill Clinton took office, "Hillary Rodham Clinton will set up shop in the West Wing of the White House, alongside the President's senior staff members, where she will help formulate policy on health care and other domestic issues."

From her powerful perch in the West Wing, Hillary set about creating a giant protective bubble around the Clinton co-presidency. She tried to fire the entire staff of White House ushers, and replace them with people she knew and trusted.

"When she realized she would have to live with the current crop of ushers whether she liked it or not, she placed restrictions on their access to the family quarters," I wrote in *The Truth about Hillary.* "During the day, they were allowed to bring important papers—such as resumes of Supreme Court nominees and other applicants for high office—directly to the Big Girl [the nickname bestowed on her by her staff], who signed off on all White House appointments. But once the president and first lady retired for the night, the ushers had orders to leave messages on a table outside the elevator, where the doors of the residence were firmly shut."

In addition, Hillary tried to move the White House press corps out of their quarters in the West Wing and into the Old Executive Office Building. When that scheme failed, she had the pressroom sealed off from the rest of the West Wing.

She ordered the installations of bedside telephones that did not go through the White House switchboard so that she and Bill could talk on encrypted phone lines without having to worry that someone was listening in.

During Bill Clinton's first hundred days, Hillary's staff began to worry that their boss was paranoid. How else could they explain her pathological suspicion of everyone around her? Some longtime Clinton critics—of which I counted myself—sought an explanation in Hillary's psychology. We speculated that Hillary's protective bubble was designed to hide deep-seated feelings that she was flawed and imperfect—feelings that had been instilled in her by her sadistic father.

Dee Dee Myers, Bill Clinton's former press secretary, agreed. "In her personal life," said Myers, "she's always seemed like she had something to hide. She had a difficult father, and she spent a lot of time trying to create an image of a functional family when she could have said, 'It's my family.' The burden of perfection was upon her, and she carried it into her marriage. There's always this fear of letting people see what they already know."

Whatever her motives, Hillary's bubble served as an effective political tool. "It camouflaged the moral decay in the Clinton White House, and misled many people into believing that the Clintons were the victims of their political adversaries, rather than the other way around," I wrote in *The Truth about Hillary*. "It helped deflect Kenneth Starr's quest for the truth about Whitewater, and left him sputtering in frustration."

After vowing never to have anything to do with the media, Hillary relented and in 1994 held what came to be known as her "pretty-in-pink" press conference (so called because she wore a pink sweater set). Seated before a group of reporters in the White House State Dining Room, she spent an hour and twelve minutes defending the indefensible—her $99,000 overnight profit on a $1,000 investment in commodities trading.

How did a novice accomplish such a financial feat?

"I talked to other people and read the *Wall Street Journal*," she said.

Nobody believed her.

Then came Monica Lewinsky and Hillary's preposterous version of what she knew and when she knew it.

In her memoir *Living History*, Hillary claimed that Bill woke her in their bedroom and "told me for the first time that there had been an inappropriate intimacy" with Monica Lewinsky. "I could hardly breathe," she wrote. "Gulping for air, I started crying and yelling at him."

"The fact of the matter was," I wrote in *The Truth about Hillary*, "Hillary knew everything—and she knew it before anybody else. And yet, she never changed her tune. Even after the truth about Bill and Monica came out, Hillary continued to defend her husband.... In a gesture that was meant to rally the Clintons' African American base, Hillary invited the Reverend Jesse Jackson to the White House to 'counsel' the First Family.... The Reverend Jackson held a press conference and—perhaps inadvertently, perhaps not—demolished Hillary's gulping-for-air story.... 'Hillary's not naïve,' Jesse Jackson said. 'There was no great explosive shock and surprise moment. Hillary knew her husband well and has for twenty-five years. The best evidence of that is that Sunday as the drama was building, she was organizing his testimony, and she knew what was going on.'"

The casualty toll during the Clintons' White House years from Hillary's secrecy, lying, and obfuscation was staggering:

- Many Clinton friends went to jail. Fifteen of them—including Whitewater partners Jim and Susan McDougal, White House counsel Webster Hubbell, and Arkansas Governor Jim Guy Tucker—were convicted of federal charges.
- Hillary was hauled before a grand jury, the first time in American history that a first lady had been subpoenaed to testify.
- Vince Foster, Hillary's closest friend in the White House, was dead, a suicide.
- The House of Representatives approved two articles of impeachment against Bill Clinton, charging him with lying under oath about his sexual relationship with Monica Lewinsky.

- After Bill Clinton perjured himself in the Lewinsky scandal, he lost his Arkansas law license and was disbarred from practicing before the Supreme Court.

━━━━

Fast forward four decades to the State Department inspector general's blistering report about Hillary's hazardous use of an unsecure email server, and nothing had changed. Nothing, that is, except that this time the liberal mainstream media could not ignore the truth about Hillary, although they did everything in their power to sugarcoat the fact that she had put her selfish interests before her country's national security.

"Hillary Clinton's campaign for the presidency just got harder with the release of the State Department inspector general's finding that 'significant security risks' were posed by her decision to use a private email server for personal and official business while she was secretary of state," the *New York Times* editorialized.

Translated from Times-*speak: The hardships Hillary imposed on her campaign were more important than the security risks she imposed on America.*

USA Today chimed in: "If Clinton wants to become the president of the United States, she needs to explain how she could make such a reckless decision."

She got some "splainin" to do! That would clear up everything.

On an MSNBC panel, Mike Barnicle said the report "adds to the weight of voter exhaustion when it comes to the Clintons."

We're exhausted with the Clintons, but not ready to abandon them.

Less than two weeks after the IG released the report, Hillary won the New Jersey and California primaries, cinching the Democratic nomination. Several days later, President Obama released a YouTube video in which he gave Hillary his full-throated endorsement.

"I don't think there's ever been someone so qualified to hold this office," said Obama.

Putting aside the small detail that at least a half dozen more qualified people had blessed the office of president—George Washington, Thomas Jefferson, Abraham Lincoln, Franklin Roosevelt, Dwight Eisenhower, and Ronald Reagan—Obama ignored an even more pertinent fact: Hillary Clinton was the first presumptive nominee of a major political party who was under criminal investigation by the FBI.

And as he sought to lay the cornerstone of his legacy, Barack Obama had to deal with that unforgivably cringeworthy reality.

PART 9

RUNNING

OUT

OF TIME

To cover-up her corrupt dealings, Hillary Clinton illegally stashed her State Department emails on a private server. Her server was easily hacked by foreign governments—perhaps even by her financial backers in Communist China—putting all of America in danger. Then there are the 33,000 emails she deleted. While we may not know what is in those deleted emails, our enemies probably do. So they probably now have a blackmail file over someone who wants to be President of the United States. This fact alone disqualifies her from the Presidency.

—Donald J. Trump, June 22, 2016

CHAPTER
27

Too Big to Fail

arack Obama's endorsement of Hillary sent a clear and unmistakable message: she was not going to be indicted. The president's seal of approval, wrote columnist Michael Goodwin, "was a virtual 'all clear' signal to the Justice Department as well as to hesitant Democratic voters."

Most people who were familiar with how Washington works agreed with Goodwin. Look, they said, everyone knows Hillary is guilty as sin: she sent and received classified information on an unsecure email server that was hackable by America's enemies; she indulged in pay-to-play shenanigans with the Clinton Foundation when she was secretary of state; and her top aides suffered a sudden onset of amnesia when they testified under oath, suggesting that Hillary had conspired to suborn witnesses. Yet despite all that, Hillary would never pay for her crimes, because the president of the United States wouldn't let that happen.

Doubts that Hillary would receive the fate she deserved were compounded by the interminable FBI investigation. At the time of Obama's endorsement of Hillary on June 9, the criminal inquiry had been dragging on for almost fourteen months, and to hear FBI Director James Comey tell it, there appeared to be no end in sight. Even if the FBI ultimately recommended that Hillary be prosecuted, said the skeptics, it beggared the imagination that Attorney General Loretta Lynch—a Democratic prosecutor appointed by a Democratic president—would follow through by empaneling a grand jury and asking for indictments.

Conservatives in particular scoffed at the idea that Lynch would uphold the ideal that everyone is equal in the eyes of the law. They doubted that Comey would dare destabilize the political system by releasing the rap sheet of a major party nominee. And they dismissed the notion that Obama would sabotage his party and legacy by throwing his likely successor to the wolves.

Hillary, they concluded, was too big to fail.

∎

Curiously enough, one person who did not share this view of untrammeled presidential power was Barack Obama. After seven and a half years of bumping heads with Congress and the courts, he subscribed to Harry Truman's sardonic view of presidential power. When contemplating General Eisenhower winning the presidential election of 1952, Truman said, "He'll sit here, and he'll say, 'Do this! Do that!' *And nothing will happen.* Poor Ike—it won't be like the Army. He'll find it very frustrating."

No one frustrated Obama more than "Big Jim" Comey. The two men didn't see eye to eye on anything, and their clash over the investigation of Hillary Clinton had the makings of a showdown. By the middle of June, a White House source was describing Obama as "at his wit's end" with Comey.

"The president made every effort to give Comey all the time he reasonably needed to wrap things up," said the source, who spoke on the condition of anonymity because of the sensitive nature of the discussions between Obama and Comey. "But Comey continued to throw a huge chunk of the FBI's badly stretched resources at the Hillary investigation. Obama thinks Comey is obsessed with the case, and that Comey has a burr up his butt about Hillary.

"Obama tried everything, including a charm offensive," the source continued. "But his magic didn't work. Obama sensed a lot of hostility in Comey, and that made him steaming mad. He believed Comey and his agents were completely out of control, and had a right-wing Republican agenda. He got so mad at Comey that sometimes he didn't make sense. I've actually heard Obama say that Comey was trying to capture the White House through a legal coup. Obama's endorsement of Hillary was a clear signal to Comey that it was time to wise up."

But Comey was unbudgeable. And with the Democratic National Convention only weeks away, Obama turned to his last line of defense: Loretta Lynch. In late June, Obama and Valerie Jarrett had a come-to-Jesus meeting with Lynch in the Oval Office.

"It's your responsibility to keep this thing from spiraling out of control," Obama told Lynch, according to Jarrett's description of the meeting, which she shared with a source for this book. "Do *something*!"

The spectacle of Barack Obama going to bat for Hillary Clinton raised questions among readers of my books. They sent me emails and text messages demanding to know "what happened to that blood feud you wrote about?"

And indeed, in my 2014 book *Blood Feud: The Clintons vs. the Obamas*, I had written:

> Not since the feud between Ted Kennedy and Jimmy Carter tore apart the Democratic Party more than thirty years earlier had two pillars of the political establishment loathed each other quite as much as Bill Clinton and Barack Obama.... The rival Clinton and Obama clans had been at war with each other ever since the bruising 2008 presidential primary campaign, when Obama's surrogates tarred and feathered Bill Clinton for being a "racist," and a Clinton aide mocked Barack Obama for embracing "the politics of trash" ... This was a family fight, and as the saying goes, no one fights dirtier or more brutally than blood.

The loathing Obama felt for the Clintons hadn't changed since then. As far as Obama was concerned, Bill was still "ruthless, dishonest and constantly scheming," and Hillary "couldn't be trusted" (Obama's words). What had changed, however, were the circumstances in which Obama found himself as he neared the end of his term in office.

When he left the White House on January 20, 2017, Obama would be fifty-five years old, a relatively young man who, health permitting, could look forward to another quarter century of active political life. He desperately wanted to stay in the thick of things, and planned to remain in Washington, the first former president since Woodrow Wilson to live in the nation's capital after leaving the White House.

He and Michelle rented a mansion from Joe Lockhart, a former Clinton press secretary who recently became the top public relations official of the National Football League, in the Kalorama section of Washington, just down the street from the French Embassy. It was a three-story brick Tudor with nine bedrooms and eight and a half baths. There was plenty of room for the entire Obama entourage—Valerie Jarrett; Michelle's mother, Marian Robinson; the two Obama girls, Sasha, fifteen, a junior at Sidwell Friends School, and Malia, eighteen, who was taking a year off before enrolling in Harvard; aides, secretaries, butlers, maids, and cooks; and the Secret Service detail. There was a terrace with gardens and parking for ten cars—a major luxury in downtown D.C.

"The house sold a few years ago for $5 million, and Valerie assumes the Obamas are going to buy it and stay in D.C. permanently," said a source close to Jarrett. "The Secret Service has already inspected the house and the grounds, and is planning to install bullet-proof windows and everything that needs to be done to protect the former first family.

"Valerie met with Rupert Murdoch to talk about a deal with HarperCollins [one of the world's largest publishing companies], which is owned by Murdoch's News Corp.," the source continued. "They shook hands on giving HarperCollins the first rights to negotiate an offer for a multiple book deal—one by Michelle, one by Valerie, and possibly three by Barack.

"Valerie said she was completely charmed by Murdoch, and hopes the deal works out, because he assured her that he would personally see to it that the books were handled right and became international bestsellers. Obviously, Barack and Michelle have been on the opposite side of the political fence from Murdoch, who's a staunch conservative, but neither of them had any objection to going with HarperCollins if things worked out financially. They are talking of book advances in the neighborhood of $100 million—the biggest deal in publishing history.

"In addition to books, the Obamas are also talking about a documentary film for theatrical release that would chronicle the rise of an African American man from humble beginnings to the world's highest office. Valerie and Barack have talked to Steven Spielberg about the idea, and Spielberg is very enthusiastic about it. He wants to play a role in putting the documentary together, perhaps as executive producer. With Spielberg behind it, the documentary could be a major cultural event and win all kinds of awards, including an Academy Award."

According to White House press secretary Josh Earnest, Obama was interested in owning an NBA franchise.

"Barack has wanted to be an owner or part owner of a professional basketball team for years," said a close associate of Valerie Jarrett. "As soon as he became president he knew he was going to make many millions on books and speeches, and he could finally make his dream come true. He is more than a fan. He knows the players like an owner would. He knows where they came from, their stats, their strengths and weaknesses.

"Valerie and Michelle threw a little cold water on the basketball idea," the source continued. "They joked that people would compare him to George W. Bush, who was co-owner of the Texas Rangers. Valerie questioned whether investing tens of millions in a sports franchise was necessarily a wise investment. She promised to gather a team of expert sports financial analysts to advise if Barack decides to go ahead with it."

For his post-presidency, Obama had originally tried to establish a line of succession in the Democratic Party that excluded the Clintons. Given the chance, he would have happily endorsed either Joe Biden or Elizabeth Warren. He had no doubt that if either of them won the election, they would have shown him proper gratitude, treated him with deep respect, and welcomed him into the governing councils of the Democratic Party. He would have been more than a former president; he would have been president emeritus.

But neither Biden nor Warren were ready to take the leap into presidential politics, and after a lot of argument and arm-twisting by Valerie Jarrett, Obama finally faced reality: he was stuck with Hillary Clinton. He knew he wouldn't get the kid-glove treatment from Hillary that he would have gotten from Biden or Warren, but the Obama-Clinton blood feud no longer made political sense.

After their bitterly fought 2008 primary contest, Hillary had endorsed Obama and helped him unite the Democratic Party. For that and other reasons, Obama had appointed her secretary of state. Now, it was Hillary's turn to make an offer in return for Obama's endorsement. Over the course of several meetings in the White House, Hillary promised Obama the moon and the stars. He could have anything he wanted, she said, including a seat on the Supreme Court.

"The idea of looking cool in a black robe and becoming a justice of the Supreme Court intrigued Obama," said a White House source close to Jarrett. "But Valerie told him he was living in fantasy land. Even when he was teaching constitutional law at the University of Chicago, he never really liked the quiet professorial life. He likes action, worshipful crowds, and swooning women.

"What made more sense to Valerie was for Obama to become a roving super-ambassador," the source added. "That was more his speed. He was beloved around the world and he loves the adulation. He likes the idea of playing the Henry Kissinger role, negotiating with the Chinese and the Russians, sorting out the big issues that confront the world, and showing everybody how smart he is.

"But whatever he does in the future, Obama first intends to campaign against Donald Trump as if he's running for a third term. The idea of Trump and a band of barbarians taking over the White House, trampling on his legacy, and destroying every-thing he's done over the past eight years is abhorrent to him. He has never forgotten that Trump questioned whether he was born in the United States. Trump challenged his right to be president. Trump called Obama's identity into question. And he hated Don-ald Trump more than he ever hated Bill Clinton."

———

"We were having dinner in the dining room of the Family Residence at the White House and the subject of Hillary's health came up," said a source close to the Obamas. "Valerie pointed out that Hillary's campaign schedule was highly unusual in that she was taking a great number of days off. Clearly, she doesn't have the energy to go nearly full time, which is what Barack did when he was campaigning. Hillary just doesn't have the stamina for it.

"If Hillary wasn't up against a candidate who is his own worst enemy, she would be in serious trouble," the source continued. "But still the polling shows there is a lack of enthusiasm for Hill-ary and that the election is not going to be a slam dunk for her.

"Over dinner, Valerie, Barack, and Michelle speculated that if Hillary won the presidency, she could become incapacitated during her term in office. Barack said that he intended to cam-paign with a vengeance for her, first because the idea of a Trump presidency is appalling, but also because he wants Hillary to owe him big time. All three said they could envision Hillary becoming ill due to her health issues and the extreme pressure she would be under as president. Then she would need help, and they would be just up Connecticut Avenue, and more than willing to come to her aid.

"Valerie laughed and said that it could become like the Woodrow Wilson scenario; after President Wilson had a stroke, his wife Edith virtually ran the government for more than a year.

"They all agreed that, healthwise, Bill would be in no position to run the country. And Chelsea could be brushed aside. They were all gleeful about the idea of keeping their hands on the levers of power and running the country from their new home in Kalorama."

CHAPTER
28

Fort Hoover

66 I was having a Fourth of July party in my backyard when I got word that Jim [Comey], his wife Patrice, and three of his children were going to drop by," said one of Comey's neighbors in McLean, Virginia, who was also one of his closest friends. "Jim showed up in a big motorcade of black SUVs with a whole bunch of uniformed agents in yellow FBI shirts. He accepted a beer in a cup and a hot dog, which he only partially ate. He walked around the party, greeting friends, but after about fifteen minutes, he thanked me and took off in his SUV. I knew where he was going because he told me. He was going to FBI headquarters to put the finishing touches on the speech he planned to deliver on television the next day about the Hillary email investigation.

"We had discussed the pressure he was under and how he was handling it," his friend continued. "He'd been under attack for months from all sides—the political Left and Right—and he'd been getting rumblings of discontent from within the Bureau. His top deputies were telling him to shit or get off the pot. They were getting so much incoming fire from the White House and Democrats in Congress that they'd started calling the FBI building Fort Hoover."

As Americans celebrated Independence Day, Comey's agents and technical specialists weren't free to eat hot dogs and sip beers. They were holed up in Fort Hoover collecting more evidence and piecing together the information they already had in hand. However, as far as the rest of the intelligence community was concerned, Comey's troops were on their own. Whenever officials of the FBI asked for help from their colleagues in the CIA, NSA, or DIA, they got the same answer: "We can't find a single thing on Hillary."

"The Intel people were simply not on board," said a source close to Comey. "They were convinced that Hillary was going to win the election and become the next commander in chief, and they didn't want to get on her wrong side."

What stung the most was the lack of cooperation from the National Security Agency, which each day recorded billions of phone calls, emails, and social media messages through electronic signals intelligence. Presumably, Hillary's emails—including the ones she erased—were among the NSA's metadata.

"We...know that Clinton disregarded NSA's repeated warnings against the use of unencrypted communications," wrote Ray McGovern, a former CIA analyst who had prepared the president's daily intelligence briefing and chaired a group on the National Intelligence Council that produced National Intelligence Estimates. "One of the NSA's core missions, after all, is to create and maintain secure communications for military, diplomatic, and other government users.

"Clinton's flouting of the rules, in NSA's face, would have created additional incentives for NSA to keep an especially close watch on her emails and telephone calls," McGovern continued. "The NSA also might know whether some foreign intelligence service successfully hacked into Clinton's server."

Help arrived at Fort Hoover from an unexpected source—Julian Assange, the Australian computer programmer who founded WikiLeaks.

Assange was a wanted man. He was living in Ecuador's London embassy, which had granted him asylum to shield him from extradition to Sweden, where he was wanted for questioning in connection with an alleged rape. He relished his celebrity and gave frequent interviews from the safety of the Ecuadorian embassy. Speaking to a British TV reporter, he promised to publish a trove of Hillary's emails that would contain enough evidence to indict her.

"We have upcoming leaks in relation to Hillary Clinton," said Assange. "We've accumulated a lot of material about Hillary Clinton. We could proceed to an indictment.... There's very strong material both in the emails and in relation to the Clinton Foundation."

"Although Assange is prone to flights of fancy," wrote John Schindler, a former National Security Agency analyst and counterintelligence officer, "WikiLeaks has long served as a front for Russian intelligence, as Western security services are well aware, so it may not be fantasy that he could get his hands on more of Hillary's emails. It would be supremely ironic if the Kremlin demolished Hillary Clinton's presidential aspirations thanks to her own neglect of basic communications security when she was secretary of state."

■■■

Though Comey often reminded his top deputies that he didn't want to be rushed into making a decision, they had recently been warning him that he was running out of time. They hardly needed to remind him that the outcome of the presidential race could hinge on the FBI investigation. It was time for action, they said.

Aware of these growing rumblings of discontent in his ranks, Comey assembled eight of his top deputies—men and women he had worked with for years and whose judgment he trusted. All eight urged him to wrap up the investigation as soon as possible and make his referral.

"Things started moving fast," said an FBI source. "The remaining piece of the puzzle was getting Hillary to sit down at FBI headquarters for an interview."

CHAPTER
29

"A Perfect Storm of Misery"

While all this was going on, Omar Mateen, a former armed guard employed by a private security firm (his most recent assignment had been as an unarmed security guard at a retirement home), slaughtered forty-nine people in a gay nightclub in Orlando, Florida—the worst mass murder in U.S. history. The American-born son of Afghan parents, with a father who was a supporter of the Taliban, Mateen had popped up on the FBI's watch list twice for expressing radical Islamic sympathies, and twice he had slipped through the FBI's fingers.

After the killings, the owner of a Jensen Beach, Florida, gun shop said that he had reported to authorities that Mateen—whom he described as a suspicious man of Middle Eastern descent—tried to buy body armor and bulk ammunition. However, no one followed up on the tip. Given these and other signs that Mateen was both an Islamic State–inspired terrorist and was psychologically unbalanced (which was evident to some of his former colleagues), questions were raised about the FBI's failure to stop him before it was too late.

The FBI's fumble in Orlando offered the dirty tricksters in the Clinton Slime Room—David Brock, Philippe Reines, and Sidney Blumenthal—the chance to attack James Comey. Multi-million-dollar Super PACs like Correct the Record and David Brock's American Bridge charged that Comey was wasting the FBI's resources persecuting Hillary rather than going after terrorists.

"Sid [Blumenthal] was the Rasputin in the campaign against Comey," a source close to the Clintons said in an interview for this book. "He was in touch with Hillary daily. Here she was, finally within reach of the goal she'd been pursuing all her life—the White House—and this son of a bitch Comey was trying to steal it from her. Sid was her secret agent in the fight.

"She told him to do whatever it took to cripple Comey," the source continued, "but she didn't want to know the details, because she was going to be interviewed by the FBI, and it was going to be hard enough to get through that without having to lie about Sid's black-ops work.

"Sid loves email because he thinks he's a great writer. But ever since the *Times* broke Hillary's email scandal way back in the spring of 2015, the Clintons had a pact—no incendiary ideas of any kind should be put in the form of an email, which could easily be hacked. So Sid had to pass his ideas around verbally to the men who were in charge of the slash-and-burn campaign against Comey."

Asked by PBS *NewsHour*'s Judy Woodruff about the Brock-Blumenthal-Reines opposition research campaign, Hillary said, "I have no knowledge of what they are doing."

As usual, lying came easily to her.

"Hillary turned crimson in the face when she talked about Comey," said a source who spent a lot of time with Hillary. "When she got angry like that, she braced herself against a wall or a chair or any nearby object, like she'd lost her balance and was going to fall down. It worried me a lot. Her doctor examined her daily and constantly monitored her vital signs. He kept a close watch, and if she got light headed, he was there to grab her.

"She told me she'd come close to falling down when she got overly tired," the source continued. "She took frequent naps to avoid an episode of fainting like she had when she was at the State Department. The coughing fits also seemed to happen when she was worn down. It was painful to see her go through that. Fortunately, it happened a lot less in public than it did in private.

"But despite all the stress she was under, I don't think she ever uttered the words 'If I'm indicted.' That would be negative thinking, and Hillary doesn't engage in that."

Hillary was a smart lawyer and a disciplined politician, and she never once let on in public how angry and vulnerable she felt as a result of the FBI investigation. She stuck to her false story that nothing marked classified ever passed across her server. She ridiculed those who said she had jeopardized national security. In classic Clinton fashion, she parsed words and said that her political opponents were misrepresenting the State Department inspector general's report, which criticized her for failing to seek approval for her use of a private email server and for ignoring rules for preserving public records. In sum, she acted as though she hadn't been caught in what one critic called "a perfect storm of misery."

When Jorge Ramos of Univision asked her at a Democratic debate whether she would drop out of the presidential race if the FBI investigation produced an indictment, she dismissed the question as absurd.

"For goodness sake," she said, "that is not gonna happen. I'm not even answering that question."

She repeated the mantra in an interview with Fox News' Bret Baier. "That is not going to happen," she said. "There is no basis for it, and I'm looking forward to this being wrapped up as soon as possible."

> **Baier:** Very last thing. The Clinton Foundation investigation, the FBI investigation into the email, you're saying zero chance that this is a problem for you. In this election.

Clinton: Absolutely. That's what I'm saying. That happens
to be the truth.

Some legal experts in academia, where Hillary was popular
among progressive professors, used a jumble of meaningless
words to support her claims of innocence.

"I believe Clinton did break the law but at the same time I
don't think there's evidence she committed a crime," said Douglas
Cox, associate professor at City University of New York Law
School.

But sophists like Professor Cox were in the minority.

"I don't think there's any question Mrs. Clinton and her staff
broke the law," said Joseph DiGenova, a former federal prosecutor. "She maintained a server in her private home in Chappaqua,
New York, and conducted government business. This clearly was
beyond gross negligence. When she set up the server, the intent
was to avoid accountability. There is no other intent required. The
notion this is not a violation of the law is ludicrous."

CHAPTER
30

"From the Political Frying Pan to the Fire"

On the morning of July 5, when James Comey strode into the FBI auditorium to address the nation on his exhaustive, sixteen-month-long investigation of Hillary Clinton, it was obvious to practically everyone in America that Hillary was guilty as sin. But whether she was "prosecutable"—that is, whether a jury was likely to find her guilty of her sins—was an entirely different matter. Normally, that matter did not fall within the purview of the FBI director. During the 108 years of its existence, the job of the FBI had always been to gather the facts in a criminal investigation and then turn them over to prosecutors in the Justice Department to decide whether to bring charges.

However, as far as Comey was concerned, nothing about this investigation was normal. To wit:

- Bill Clinton had thoroughly contaminated the non-political nature of the investigation by barging onto the private jet of Attorney General Loretta Lynch— technically, Comey's boss—making it look like the outcome was rigged.
- The president of the United States had conducted a sub rosa campaign to obstruct the probe by directing the intelligence community not to cooperate with the FBI.
- Senate Minority Leader Harry Reid and House Minority Leader Nancy Pelosi had accused Comey of waging a hysterical campaign to prevent Hillary from becoming president.
- Democrats in Congress had begun referring to Comey as Captain Queeg, the mentally unhinged skipper in Herman Wouk's novel *The Caine Mutiny*.
- Republicans had called for Hillary's head on a plate.
- Conservatives had decided that the whole thing was rigged.

On July 2, three days before Comey's appearance, Hillary came to FBI headquarters for an interview. It was not recorded or transcribed, but according to those who were permitted to read the FBI notes of the three-and-a-half-hour interview (which contained highly classified information), Hillary parried the questions with lawyerly answers. Comey would later say that she had not lied to the FBI, but it soon became apparent that Crooked Hillary was up to her old tricks.

She falsely claimed to the FBI that former Secretary of State Colin Powell had advised her to use a personal email account. *It was all Colin Powell's fault!* That same day, however, Powell forcefully denied the story.

"The truth is, she was using [the private email server] for a year before I sent her a memo telling her what I did," Powell said. "Her people have been trying to pin it on me."

Over the Fourth of July weekend, Comey sought advice from legal scholars, judges, and old friends. By far, most thought he should not recommend an indictment. If Hillary eventually skated, they warned him, he could harm the reputation of the FBI and ruin his career.

In the end, according to his friends who were interviewed for this book, Comey turned to the person he trusted most—his wife Patrice.

"He's a deeply religious guy, an Evangelical Catholic, and he and Patrice prayed together on their knees, asking for God's guidance," said a source close to both Comeys. "Patrice told him that he was cracking under the pressure, and that he had to move on and make a decision one way or the other. He said that it was Pat's concern about how his personal anguish was having an effect

on his family that was the determining factor. He decided he had
to take full responsibility. He couldn't leave it up to the prosecutors."

His decision not to recommend an indictment brought a torrent of criticism.

"Mr. Comey didn't explain why, with evidence clearly fulfill-
ing the requirements of the two statutes involved, no reasonable
prosecutor would bring a case—except for the director's inac-
curate assertion that it had never been done before," wrote
Michael B. Mukasey, who served as U.S. attorney general under
President George W. Bush. "It may be that someday there will be
the usual transparency: disclosure of facts. That day was not
Tuesday, and it is little wonder that many in and out of government were left both puzzled and dismayed."

Investor's Business Daily was even harsher in its judgment:
"It is now evident that the FBI fumbled its investigation into Hillary Clinton's misuse of a private email server while serving as
secretary of state. It found evidence of crimes but refused to
prosecute. Whether it was dereliction, incompetence or something
far more sinister are the only real questions that remain to be
answered.... It is now clear the meeting between President Bill
Clinton and Attorney General Loretta Lynch last week was a
premeditated attempt at cooking justice—making sure that neither the Justice Department nor the FBI, which is part of the

Justice Department, would recommend charges against what were plainly illegal acts by Hillary Clinton."

The Hill put it more succinctly: "James Comey went from the political frying pan to the fire."

At first, Comey told his deputies that he regretted his decision; he should have nailed Hillary. But in the days that followed, he came to a different conclusion, one that rationalized his decision to let Hillary go free and that made him feel virtuous.

"Jim ultimately considered the investigation into the Clinton emails something of a success," said a source close to the FBI director. "By indicting her politically if not legally, he showed that she is not a person who should be trusted. Had he asked for and gotten an indictment and a jury had found her not guilty, there would be headlines declaring her not guilty. But this way, that's not going to happen. She is not going to get the opportunity to claim that the FBI was on a partisan witch-hunt. And she is not off the hook. The FBI investigation into her trading government favors for cash donations to the Clinton Foundation—that's going full blast and will almost certainly lead to another public excoriation."

CHAPTER
31

"In This to the End"

With the approach of Labor Day and the start of the political season, Hillary pulled ahead of Donald Trump by several points in most election polls. FiveThirtyEight, a website that uses statistical analysis to predict the outcome in politics and sports, gave Hillary a 78.8 percent chance of winning the election. Many political observers concluded that Trump had inflicted severe wounds on himself by, among other things, insulting a Gold Star family, accusing Hillary and Obama of "founding" ISIS, and urging "Second Amendment people" to go after Hillary (which was interpreted by the mainstream media as encouraging assassination).

But then something totally unexpected happened: the Associated Press ran a bombshell story that was a game changer.

It reported that "more than half the people outside the government who met with Hillary Clinton when she was secretary of
state gave money—either personally or through companies or
groups—to the Clinton Foundation." What's more, "at least 85
of 154 people from private interests who met or had phone conversations scheduled with Clinton while she led the State Department donated to her family charity or pledged commitments to
its international programs."

There were several reasons that the AP story had the potential
to alter the trajectory of the presidential campaign, making it
much more of a horse race.

First, although many of the AP's reporters are card-carrying
members of the liberal mainstream media, the wire service has the
reputation of striving for balance and fairness in its political coverage. Unlike the *New York Times*, it is not a house organ for the
Democratic Party and Hillary Clinton, and therefore its Clinton
Foundation investigation carried a lot of weight and credibility.

Second, until the AP story, remarkably enough FBI Director
James Comey had been unaware of the extent of Hillary's meetings with non-government individuals; he did not know, for
instance, that the eighty-five people mentioned in the AP story
had contributed $156 million to the Clinton Foundation.

And third, the AP story lit a fire under the FBI's ongoing investigation into Hillary's pay-to-play relationship with the foundation.

"As soon as he got wind of the AP story, Comey called a meeting
of his top deputies," said a retired Justice Department official with
unimpeachable sources inside the FBI. "I talked to two men who were
at the meeting, and they said that Comey was in high dudgeon,

because a wire service had stolen a march on the FBI. He paced the floor as he instructed his deputies to release the thirty-page investigative report on Hillary's emails that he sent to the Justice Department as well as the twelve-page copy of the notes taken during Hillary's FBI interview. And he ordered his deputies to redouble their efforts to uncover the link between Hillary and donors to her family foundation.

"In particular," this source continued, "the FBI is trying to determine if Hillary had a separate and secret schedule of meetings with foreign governments and private industry figures who were making sizable contributions to the foundation. The question wasn't whether donors sought access to the secretary of state; people who donate money are always given special access to political figures. That's always been part of our political system and, though it might sound corrupt, it isn't considered criminal.

"The real question was whether foundation donors were given favors by Hillary that helped put money in their pockets. That kind of quid pro quo is illegal. And under Comey's prodding, FBI agents started turning up testimony that Hillary offered those quid pro quos on numerous occasions."

To kick the FBI's investigation of the foundation into high gear, Comey ordered the release to Congress of nearly 15,000 work-related emails that Hillary had failed to turn over to the State Department. The 14,900 deleted emails—including 30 related to Benghazi—had been forensically recovered from Hillary's server and other sources. Among other things, the new emails revealed:

- Doug Band, one of Bill Clinton's closest associates who helped create the Clinton Foundation, wrote to Huma

Abedin that Crown Prince Salman bin Hamad al-Khalifa of Bahrain, who had donated $32 million to the Clinton Global Initiative, was seeking a meeting with Secretary of State Clinton. "Asking to see her," Band wrote Abedin on behalf of the crown prince. "Good friend of ours." A couple of days later, Abedin informed Band that the crown prince was scheduled to see Hillary. "If u see him let him know," she emailed. "We have reached out thru official channels."

- Band asked Abedin to help out a big foundation donor who was trying to secure a visa for a British soccer player facing criminal charges.

- Another Bill Clinton aide, Ben Schwerin, emailed Abedin and Band asking for a favor for U2's Bono, who had contributed to the Clinton Global Initiative. "Bono wants to do linkup with the international space station on every show during his tour this year," Schwerin wrote Abedin and Band.

- Cheryl Mills, Hillary's chief of staff at the State Department, was so intimately involved in Clinton Foundation business that she and Laura Graham, the foundation's chief operating officer, exchanged 148 telephone messages between 2010 and 2012.

"As I watch Hillary Clinton wish away the fallout of the Clinton Foundation's unseemly ties with the State Department during her tenure as secretary of state, I can't help but think that her self-inflicted wound just bleeds and bleeds and bleeds," wrote

Elise Jordan, an NBC News/MSNBC political analyst who previously worked for the Department of State and the National Security Council. "Every day that she fails to seriously address the rotten consequences of her poor judgment, Clinton further erodes the already lacking public trust in her.... The fact that Clinton has not given a press conference in 264 days is far more damaging than the seeming corruption itself. If she didn't do anything wrong, why won't she defend herself?"

Many Republicans in Congress believed they knew the answer to that question: Hillary couldn't defend herself because she had lied through her teeth. Jason Chaffetz, chairman of the House Oversight Committee, and Bob Goodlatte, chairman of the Judiciary Committee, demanded Hillary be charged with perjury for lying to the FBI and lying under oath to Congress.

"The evidence collected by the Federal Bureau of Investigation (FBI) during its investigation of Secretary of State Clinton's use of a personal email system during her time as Secretary of State appears to directly contradict several aspects of her sworn testimony," Chaffetz and Goodlatte wrote in a letter to Channing Phillips, the U.S. attorney for the District of Columbia.

███████

Comey had not recommended an indictment on the email scandal. But the investigation continued on the Clinton Foundation and the possible corrupt dealings of Hillary Clinton as secretary of state.

There were reports in the media that Attorney General Loretta Lynch had squelched Comey's investigation of the foundation and

rebuffed the GOP's call for a criminal inquiry into Hillary's testimony to Congress. Those reports were wrong. However, in the
wake of Comey's decision not to recommend an indictment on
the email server scandal, Lynch made it clear to Comey that if he
now decided to recommend an indictment on charges of public
corruption, the Justice Department wouldn't act until well after
the November election.

So where does that leave James Comey and his investigation
into the Clinton Foundation corruption?

Bill Clinton, still the smartest political animal around, thought
he had the answer.

"Comey's twelve years older [than he was when he threatened
to resign under [President Bush] and he's less brash," Bill said,
according to the recollection of one of his advisers who was interviewed for this book. "He's not dealing with the legality of a
warrantless wiretap program or the use of enhanced interrogation
techniques. He's dealing with the likely first woman president of
the United States. His actions will be recorded in history books.
Does he want to be remembered for all time as the guy who threw
the country into a constitutional crisis? I don't think so. I'm bet-
ting that whatever he does will be measured and legalistic."

Bill and his adviser thought that Comey would most likely
go around Loretta Lynch and take his case to Preet Bharara, the
U.S. attorney for the Southern District of New York. Bharara's

jurisdiction extended from the tip of Manhattan north to West-chester County, where Hillary has her home in Chappaqua.

"Bharara runs one of the largest and most respected offices of federal prosecutors in the country," wrote Jeffrey Toobin, the legal analyst for CNN and the *New Yorker*. "Under his leadership, the office has charged dozens of Wall Street figures with insider trad-ing, and has upended the politics of New York State, by convicting the leaders of both houses of the state legislature.... [Bharara] brought a media-friendly approach to what has historically been a closed and guarded institution. In professional background, Bhar-ara resembles his predecessors; in style, he's very different. His personality reflects his dual life in New York's political and legal firmament. A longtime prosecutor, he sometimes acts like a bud-ding pol; his rhetoric leans more toward the wisecrack than toward the jeremiad. He expresses himself in the orderly paragraphs of a former high-school debater, but with deft comic timing and a gift for shtick."

Comey and Bharara were close friends. Bharara visited Comey when he was on business in Washington, and Comey visited him in New York. Bharara frequently called on the FBI for help with his investigations of Wall Street white-collar crimes. And Comey had ordered the FBI field office in New York to work closely with Bhar-ara on his investigations of alleged corruption in the administration of Mayor Bill de Blasio. According to informed sources, Bharara and Comey had discussed the Hillary email case on several occasions. It seems likely that they must also have discussed the possibility of Hillary being indicted on charges of public corruption.

If Bharara agreed to prosecute the Hillary case, he would bring it to Loretta A. Preska, the chief judge of the United States District Court for the Southern District of New York. She would assign the case to one of the Southern District's forty-four judges, who in turn would then empanel a grand jury either in Manhattan or in White Plains, the county seat and commercial hub of Westchester County. The jury would decide whether the case against Hillary should go to trial.

⬛

"Of course, we'd do everything in our legal power to prevent the case from going to trial in the first place," said Bill Clinton's adviser. "We'd put together a Murderers' Row of lawyers and have them file a blizzard of motions to stop the case from going forward. But if it went to trial anyway, we'd try to move the case to Manhattan, where the jury pool is more heavily weighted with pro-Hillary African Americans than it is in White Plains.

"We'd file motions to dismiss prejudicial evidence, and we'd tie the case up in knots and stretch it out for as long as possible," he continued. "If the trial went badly, we'd take it to a federal court of appeals, and if that didn't work, we'd go all the way to the Supreme Court, which would likely be frozen in a four-to-four tie and send it back to the court of appeals.

"All of this would take months and months. During that time, Hillary would maintain her innocence and fight it out in court and in the court of public opinion.

"Bill agrees. He doesn't believe that voters will take this case seriously. He insists there's virtually no chance that [even now] Hillary will be indicted. But even if she is indicted, she has made it perfectly clear that she has no intention of dropping out of the presidential race. She intends to soldier on, under indictment or not, just the way Bill did when he was impeached. No matter what happens, Hillary is in this to the end."

EPILOGUE

The Choice

Hillary Clinton is unqualified to lead the United States through one of the most perilous periods in our history. Like it or not, however, she is on the ballot this November. Either Hillary or Donald Trump—two exceedingly unpopular candidates—will be our next president.

Which means we face a choice: Should we vote for someone who is fresh, bold, and untested, and who says what he believes even if we don't always like what he says and the way he says it (Donald Trump), or should we elect someone who has been under investigation for illegal or dishonest behavior during her entire public life, and who promises four—and possibly eight—more years of Obamaism (Hillary Clinton)?

For those who need time to think before answering that question, consider the devastation that Barack Obama has left in his wake, and the additional destruction that Hillary would inflict on our country:

- A feeble economy that fails to provide enough well-paying jobs to sustain a growing middle class.
- Failing schools that do not prepare our children for the upheavals in technology, globalization, communications, medicine, and financial markets.
- A mounting body count in America's cities from radical Islamic terrorists.
- A retreat overseas that has emboldened our enemies and thrown the world into chaos.
- An unsustainable national debt that will grow to $27.159 trillion by 2024, threatening our economy and national security.
- Eleven million people on disability—a number that exceeds the entire population of Greece.
- Unchecked immigration across our porous borders.
- An increase in violent crime in most major American cities.
- A drug epidemic throughout Middle America.
- The suppression of free speech on college campuses.
- Runaway political correctness that prevents us from honestly talking about and solving our common problems.

- Political gridlock in Washington that has created a crisis of confidence not only in our elected officials, but in our very system of government.
- An imperial presidency that runs roughshod over the Constitution.

There is a connection between all of these things—between America's weak response to the bloody reign of Islamic terror at home and abroad and our weak response to the reign of student "liberal fascism" on college campuses; between political gridlock in Washington and our unsustainable national debt; between the decline of the middle class and the drug epidemic spreading across America; between rising crime rates and the coarsening of America's morals and standards.

In short, there is a connection between Obamaism/Clintonism and the dangerous direction in which our county is headed. We are swiftly becoming a decadent society. Look up the word "decadent" in *Webster's Third New International Dictionary Unabridged*, and you may be shocked at how closely the definition describes contemporary American society:

> **decadent** adj. **1**: marked by decay or decline (as from an earlier condition of excellence or vitality): as **a**: characterized by self-indulgence...**b**: tending to regress: becoming less prominent.

The late Andrew Breitbart famously said that "politics is downstream from culture." What sort of culture do we have now? I laid out some of the markers in 2015 in my book *Unlikeable*, and in a year's time they have become only more pronounced or been surpassed. To wit:

- Marriage has been redefined in a way that no previous generation of Americans would have recognized—and failure to affirm the new liberal order can lead to legal punishment.
- A majority of Americans support the legalization of marijuana.
- In many communities, the police, not the criminals, are considered the problem.
- The percentage of adults who describe themselves as Christians is dropping by about a percentage point a year.
- Nearly a quarter of all Americans describe themselves as atheists, agnostic, or "nothing in particular."
- In less than thirty years non-Hispanic whites will no longer make up a majority of Americans; we will be a new people with perhaps fewer ties to traditional American values and American history.
- More than half the births to women under thirty occur outside of marriage.
- We have an electronic "celebrity culture" devoid of standards that praises Kim Kardashian for balancing a champagne glass on her rear end; that canonizes

Bruce Jenner, once the picture of masculinity, for changing his sex; and where the Summer's Eve feminine-care company runs a video on its website and YouTube showing a talking vagina.

- We are a coarser people: the average American woman now weighs the same as the average American man did in the 1960s; tattoos—once limited to sailors and members of biker gangs—now disfigure more than a third of all Americans under thirty; within living memory, men wore ties to baseball games, while today many people dress, even at work, as if in imitation of Shaggy of *Scooby-Doo*.

- According to a study from professors at Georgetown University's McDonough School of Business and the Thunderbird School of Global Management, employees are now twice as likely to experience rude behavior at an office as they were in 1998.

That, in part, is a portrait of America today.

The failure of most pundits to recognize this reality prevented them from grasping the significance of the populist revolt in both the Democratic and Republican primaries. It also kept them from understanding why Bernie Sanders gave Hillary such a run for her money, and why Donald Trump captured the nomination of the Republican Party.

The time has not yet arrived for an American Gibbon to write a new *Decline and Fall*, but we are fast approaching the point of no return.

How have we reached this parlous state, and what can we do about it?

We used to turn to our great public intellectuals—men like Lionel Trilling, Daniel Bell, Daniel Patrick Moynihan, William Buckley, Sidney Hook, and Jacques Barzun—for guidance to such matters.

They are all gone now.

Do we really think that Hillary and her self-righteous left-wing advisers who reside on the east and west coasts have answers to these problems? They are so detached from the lives of everyday Americans that they neither understand nor have a workable solution for the ills that plague America.

Fortunately, before Jacques Barzun passed away four years ago at the age of 104, he left us a brilliant explanation of the turmoil that is wracking American civilization. He published what many consider his masterwork, a book called *From Dawn to Decadence: 1500 to the Present: 500 Years of Cultural Life.*

The *New York Times* headlined Barzun's obituary CULTURAL CRITIC SAW THE SUN SETTING ON THE WEST. The obituary writer noted that Barzun believed "the liquidation of 500 years of civilization" was caused "by an internal crisis in the civilization itself which...had come to celebrate nihilism and rebellion."

Like many intellectuals of his time, Barzun started off as a liberal. His conversion to conservatism took place during the student protests in the late 1960s, when a mob held the dean of Columbia College hostage and invaded the university president's office and defecated on his desk.

As Barzun pointed out, "How a revolution erupts from a commonplace event—tidal wave from a ripple—is cause for endless astonishment."

He then went on to explain:

> Manners are flouted and customs broken. Foul language and direct insult become normal, in keeping with the rest of the excitement—buildings defaced, images destroyed, shops looted. Printed sheets pass from hand to hand and are read with delight or outrage—Listen to this! Angry debates multiply about things long since settled: talk of free love, of priests marrying and monks breaking their vows, of property and wives in common, of sweeping out all evils, all corruption, all at once—all things for a new and blissful life on earth ...
>
> Voices grow shrill, parties form and adopt names or are tagged with them in derision and contempt. Again and again comes the shock of broken friendships, broken families. As time goes on "betraying the cause" is an incessant charge, and there are indeed turncoats. Authorities are bewildered, heads of institutions try threats and concessions by turns, hoping the surge of subversion will collapse like previous ones.

The presidential election of 2016 comes at a time when "a new normal" is sweeping across America, turning long-accepted standards and codes of behavior upside down and making our country a coarser, grosser, and more vulgar society. As I wrote in *Unlikeable*: "Conservatives have every reason to be alarmed by the decline in American appearance and behavior, manners and morals. Along with the Roman orator Cicero, we say, 'O tempora, o mores,' which translates to 'Alas the times and the manners.'"

Since I penned those words, things have gone downhill faster than I expected. Who could have imagined just a year or so ago that President Obama, through his Departments of Justice and Education, would instruct every public school in America to provide "suitable" bathroom and locker room facilities to match transgender students' "chosen gender identity"?

Who could have imagined that former Secretary of State Condoleezza Rice would be labeled a warmonger and be prevented from giving the commencement address at Rutgers University?

Who could have imagined that radical left-wing provocateurs would place piles of human excrement on the sidewalks of American cities and stick miniature flags in the dung proclaiming: "Shit on Trump!"

Rather than working to heal the sickness that afflicts our country, Barack Obama has been making good on his promise to "fundamentally transform" America in his liberal image. It should come as no surprise that Hillary has long had the same grandiose ambitions.

"From an early age, she dreamed of living in the White House," said Hillary's first mentor, the Reverend Don Jones, her youth group minister in Park Ridge, Illinois.

At Wellesley College, Hillary's classmates frequently talked about her becoming the first woman president of the United States. At Yale Law School, Bill Clinton joined the chorus of those who believed that Hillary had the necessary qualities to make it all the way to the White House.

"If she comes to Arkansas," he said, "it's going to be my state, my future. *She could be president someday.* She could go to any state and be elected to the Senate. If she comes to Arkansas, she'll be on my turf."

Hillary has always believed that the world would be a far better place with Hillary Rodham Clinton as president.

"What Mrs. Clinton seems in all apparent sincerity to have in mind," wrote the late Michael Kelly, "is leading the way to something on the order of a reformation: the remaking of the American way of politics, government, indeed life. A lot of people, contemplating such a task, might fall prey to self-doubts. Mrs. Clinton does not."

Sound familiar? Well, consider this: On the evening of Tuesday, June 30, 2009, Barack Obama invited nine like-minded liberal historians to have dinner with him in the Family Quarters of the White House. Obama told the historians at the table that he had come up with a slogan for his administration.

"I'm thinking of calling it 'A New Foundation,'" he said.

Doris Kearns Goodwin suggested that might not be the wisest choice of words for a motto.

"Why not?" Obama asked.

"It sounds like a woman's girdle," said Goodwin.

During dinner, one subject was foremost on Obama's mind: how he could become a "transformational" president and change the historic trajectory of America's domestic and foreign policy.

And that is exactly what he set about doing from his first day in office.

"After 2009," writes Victor Davis Hanson in *National Review*, "the regulations governing food stamps and welfare were liberalized and politicized as never before. These payouts were judged not just on whether they hurt or helped people, but also, in the Greek and Roman sense, of increasing the number of recipients so as to change political realities.... Taxes are seen now not just as a way to fund expenditures, but as a punitive tool—hence the new phraseology of 1 percent, fat cats, corporate-jet owners, you did not build that, no time to profit, at some point you've made enough money, etc. A more equal but poorer America appears to be preferable to a more affluent but less equal nation."

━━━

"I've got a pen and I've got a phone," Obama warned us, "and I can use that pen to sign executive orders that take executive actions and administrative actions that move the ball forward."

During his time in office, Obama has gone it alone, acting without congressional approval with nearly 200 executive orders and 198 presidential memoranda.

"When these two forms of directives are taken together," writes Gregory Korte in *USA Today*, "Obama is on track to take more high-level executive actions than any president since Harry

Truman battled the 'Do Nothing Congress' almost seven decades ago."

Obama has inflamed partisan politics by trampling on our system of divided government and checks and balances. With a stroke of his pen, he has:

- Made it harder to purchase guns, despite the Supreme Court's refusal to hear challenges to the Second Amendment.
- Rejected the Keystone XL pipeline, eliminating thousands of potential well-paying jobs.
- Attempted to shield millions of illegal immigrants from deportation.
- Rewritten regulations on how national secrets are classified.

The Heritage Foundation has put together a list of Obama's Top Ten Abusive Executive Actions.

1. Amending Obamacare's employer mandate, providing an unauthorized subsidy to congressional staff, and encouraging state insurance commissioners not to enforce certain requirements.
2. Inventing labor law "exemptions" in violation of the WARN Act so that workers would not receive notice of impending layoffs days before the 2012 election.
3. Waiving the mandatory work requirement under the 1996 comprehensive welfare reform law, which

required able-bodied adults to work, prepare for work, or look for work in order to receive benefits under the Temporary Assistance for Needy Families (TANF) program.

4. Ignoring a statutory deadline and refusing to consider an application related to nuclear waste storage at Yucca Mountain, which activists sought to block for years.

5. Circumventing the Senate's duty to provide advice and consent on appointments and instead making "recess" appointments in violation of Article II, Section 2 of the Constitution when the Senate was actually in session.

6. Deciding not to defend the constitutionality of the federal definition of marriage in court.

7. Implementing Common Core national standards through strings-attached waivers from the No Child Left Behind Act.

8. Intimidating Florida to stop its voter roll cleanup, which included removing ineligible voters such as noncitizens, before the 2012 election.

9. Imposing the DREAM Act by executive fiat under the guise of "prosecutorial discretion."

10. Refusing to enforce federal drug laws in states that have legalized marijuana.

If Obama's abuse of power shocks you, just wait: Hillary has promised to go even further than Obama on many issues.

"She is…intent on portraying a future Clinton presidency as less an Obama third term than Obama Plus—with a touch of her I'm-wiser-and-tougher-than-him 2008 primary message," writes Glenn Thrush in *Politico*. "Since announcing her intention to run, Clinton has declared her intention to build upon or tweak (respectfully and indirectly, of course) an ever-widening range of Obama policies, including immigration reform, tax policy, college affordability, the prosecution of Wall Street executives and health care reform, the subject of her most heated domestic policy clash with Obama eight years ago."

Or as the editorial page of the *Wall Street Journal* put it: "This attempt to restore the Clinton dynasty is no mere replay of the 1990s. This time America is being offered the familiar Clinton ethics, but without Bill Clinton's bow to center-right policy. This time we are getting the grasping and corner-cutting of the Clinton entourage with economic policies somewhere to the left of President Obama's.

"Some wishful Republicans say this is merely campaign posturing," the editorial writer continued, "and that Mrs. Clinton will move to the center and govern that way. But more likely is that the Hillary of the primaries is closer to her genuine beliefs. Long before her White House days she was widely known as a woman of the left. She tried to deliver HillaryCare in 1993, only to adopt her husband's centrist styling after the Republicans took Congress in 1994. Perhaps she would be more pragmatic in dealing with Congress than Mr. Obama has been—a low bar—but only if forced by the political mood."

The potential left-wing legacy of a Hillary Clinton presidency could be profound, especially with the highest court in the land. "Many news stories appearing as the presidential campaign began in 2015 made clear that when the next president is sworn in on January 20, 2017, three Supreme Court justices would have reached their eighties, and a fourth would be 78 years old," wrote William Voegeli, a senior editor of the *Claremont Review of Books* in an article entitled "What's at Stake."

"That the next president could replace a third of the Court before facing reelection in 2020 appeared entirely plausible," Voegeli continued, "and clearly had the potential to determine whether the Court's disposition for the next quarter-century would be fundamentally liberal or conservative."

———

If you've read your bible, you know that it teaches us that words have profound meaning. "And God said, Let there be light: and there was light" is the third verse of the first chapter in the Book of Genesis. "In the beginning was the Word" is the first verse in the opening chapter of the Gospel of John.

Everything starts with words. In fact, the difference between human beings and other animals is that we name things, and by naming them, we create meaning.

However, that's not how Barack Obama and Hillary Clinton see things. For instance, under President George W. Bush, our National Security statement declared: "The struggle against militant

Islamic radicalism is the great ideological conflict of the early years of the 21st century." Under Obama, all references to religious terms, at least those that refer to Islam, such as "Islamic extremism," have been scrubbed from our national security documents.

In the midst of his killing spree in an Orlando gay nightclub, Omar Mateen called the police and described himself as an "Islamic soldier" who owed his allegiance to Abu Bakr al-Baghdadi, the leader of the Islamic State.

Speaking in English and Arabic, Mateen told a 911 dispatcher: "Praise be to Allah, and prayers as well as peace upon the prophet of Allah."

And yet, when Obama's Justice Department got around to releasing the transcript of that conversation, the references to Islam were deleted. In an interview with Chuck Todd, the host of NBC's *Meet the Press*, Attorney General Loretta Lynch tried to justify the absurdity of taking out those words:

> **Lynch:** What we're announcing tomorrow is that the FBI is releasing a partial transcript of the killer's calls with law enforcement, from inside the club. These are the calls with the Orlando PD negotiating team, who he was, where he was…that will be coming out tomorrow and I'll be headed to Orlando on Tuesday.
>
> **Todd:** Including the hostage negotiation part of this?
>
> **Lynch:** Yes, it will be primarily a partial transcript of his calls with the hostage negotiators.
>
> **Todd:** You say partial, what's being left out?

Lynch: What we're not going to do is further proclaim this
man's pledges of allegiance to terrorist groups, and
further his propaganda.

Later, under withering criticism from House Speaker Paul
Ryan and other conservatives, Lynch reversed herself and issued
an unredacted portion of that transcript. But the damage had
been done.

"It seems clear the administration's purpose here is not to
frustrate terrorist propaganda but to further its own propaganda,"
wrote James Taranto, a columnist for the *Wall Street Journal*. "As
with Benghazi, a terror attack on President Obama's watch could
imperil Democratic prospects in November. Thus the administration has been at pains to pin the Orlando attack on armed Americans, not Islamic terrorism."

This was just the latest example of the Obama administration's use of Newspeak—the fictional language created by George
Orwell in his dystopian novel *1984*—whose aim was to distort
the meaning of language.

So we have a United States ambassador to the United Nations,
Susan Rice, who defines the al-Qaeda–linked attack on our consulate in Benghazi as a "spontaneous demonstration" caused by
an anti-Islamic video.

So we have a president who labels ISIS "the JV team."

So Obama tells ABC News that "we have contained them"
in Iraq and Syria just days before the terrorist attacks in Paris.

So we have a commander in chief who claims "this campaign
[against ISIS] at this stage is firing on all cylinders," even as his

CIA director, John Brennan, is preparing to testify before Congress that "ISIL has a large cadre of Western fighters who could potentially serve as operatives for attacks in the West."

███

Which brings us back to Hillary and her misuse of language to explain why she is running for president. The country, she proclaims, is "Ready for Hillary!" even if the majority of Americans believes she is "untrustworthy" and "a liar."

"What happened in 2008 was that Hillary's candidacy got out in front of any rationale for it," David Axelrod, Obama's former strategist, said on MSNBC's *Morning Joe*, "and the danger is that's happening again [in 2016]. You hear 'Ready for Hillary'; it's like, ready for what?"

The columnist Peggy Noonan provided the best answer to Axelrod's question.

"Hillary Clinton," wrote Noonan, "has been given a great gift by Donald Trump. She hadn't been able to explain the purpose or meaning of her candidacy. She tried out various themes and slogans, but nothing ever took or seemed real. Everything came down to *I'm Hillary and I deserve it*. But now she has it, in only three words. 'I'm not Trump.' *I may have narcissistic personality disorder, but he's got it worse and in spades. If I'm corrupt, he's more corrupt. I have poor judgment? Everything he says is poor judgment*."

So in the end it all comes down to this: Do you want to vote for a scandal-scarred politician whose policies are focus-group tested before they are announced, and whose sole rationale for running for president is that she isn't somebody else? Or do you want to elect someone who is fresh, bold and—*yes*—untested and unrestrained, who promises to clean up the Augean stables of Washington, D.C., and revive American exceptionalism?

It is a momentous choice. And it is yours.

A Note on Sources

s might be expected in this era of intense partisan rancor, my books dealing with Hillary Clinton have drawn a barrage of criticism from the Left.

Much of the criticism can be traced back to Hillary's notorious attack machine and the henchmen who run that machine.

- Hillary's book-burning flack Philippe Reines ("Killing books has always been a fun pastime," Reines once bragged).
- Her secret agent Sidney Blumenthal (nicknamed "Grassy Knoll" by reporters for his dark conspiracy theories).

- Her pasty-faced Reich minister of propaganda David Brock (of whom the less said the better).
- Her quick-on-the-draw gunslinger Brian Fallon (who tried to downgrade the FBI's criminal investigation of Hillary to a "security inquiry" until FBI Director James Comey put him straight and said, "I don't even know what that means.").

These four horsemen of the apocalypse run what *New York Times* columnist Maureen Dowd calls the Clinton "Slime Room." This is how Dowd described the Clinton Slime Room: "A $28 million cluster of media monitoring groups and oppo research organizations that are vehicles to rebut and at times discredit and threaten anyone who casts a gimlet eye at Clinton, Inc."

The Clinton Slime Room has been dishing out its sludgy boilerplate for years, and it often doesn't bother to come up with fresh ways to attack its victims. When Peter Schweizer published his book *Clinton Cash*, the Clinton Slime Room attacked him with the same words used against me ("a discredited author") and the same phrase used against my books ("a work of fiction").

More recently, the Clinton Slime Room tried to "discredit" former Secret Service officer Gary Byrne's book, *Crisis of Character*, by charging that "it joins the ranks of other 'authors' in this latest in a long line of books attempting to cash in on the election cycle." Cash in! This from the people who brought you the Clinton family slush fund, a.k.a. the Clinton Foundation, and speeches that netted Hillary and Bill anywhere from $200,000 to $500,000 a shot. As for Brian Fallon, Hillary's campaign spokesman, he is paid a reported $100,000 a year to lie about his boss's lies.

"To this day," wrote Glenn Thrush and Maggie Haberman in *Politico*, "[Hillary has] surrounded herself with media conspiracy theorists who remain some of her favorite confidants, urged wealthy allies to bankroll independent organizations tasked with knee-capping reporters perceived as unfriendly, withdrawn into a gilded shell when attacked and rolled her eyes at several generations of aides who suggested she reach out to journalists rather than just disdaining them."

Ron Fournier, the former senior political columnist and director of *National Journal*, explained the Clinton Slime Room's MO this way: "Gennifer Flowers. Cattle futures. The White House travel office. Rose Law Firm files. The Lincoln Bedroom. Monica Lewinsky. And now the Clinton Foundation. What ties these stories together is the predictable, paint-by-numbers response from the Bill and Hillary Clinton political operation. 1. Deny: Salient questions are dodged, and evidence goes missing. The stone wall is built. 2. Deflect: Blame is shifted, usually to Republicans and the media. 3. Demean: People who question or criticize the Clintons get tarred as right-wing extremists, hacks, nuts, or sluts."

███████

As the old saying goes, "If you lie down with dogs, you'll rise up with fleas," so I'm never surprised by the Clinton Slime Room's efforts to discredit me. What I do find dismaying, however, is that many mainstream reporters attack me with words and phrases that could have come straight from the mouths of Reines, Blumenthal, Brock, and Fallon—and probably did. It is no secret that the denizens of the Clinton Slime Room and members of the mainstream media are on speed-dialing terms.

Here are some Clinton Slime Room echoes from recent stories about me:

- Philip Rucker, the national political correspondent of the *Washington Post*, wrote that I was best known for "bombshell books spreading rumors and innuendo, much of it discredited, about the Clintons." Note the use of the Clinton Slime Room's favorite word: *discredited*.
- Mara Liasson, the national political correspondent for National Public Radio, wrote I was "kind of the chief Clinton conspiracy theorist out there."
- Lisa Lerer, national political reporter for the Associated Press, wrote that I was "one of Clinton's most strident critics and the author of books spreading discredited rumors about her marriage." That *discredited* word again!
- Amy Chozick and Alexandra Alter of the *New York Times* wrote that my #1 *New York Times* bestseller *Blood Feud*, which toppled Hillary's memoir *Hard Choices* from its spot atop the list, was a "barely sourced account full of implausible passages."

These journalistic put-downs might make more sense if I were a young fly-by-night reporter without an established record. But I've been a journalist for nearly six decades—seven of those years as foreign editor of *Newsweek*, ten years as the editor in chief of the *New York Times Magazine* (during which time the magazine won the first Pulitzer Prize in its history), and twenty-seven years as a contributing editor of *Vanity Fair*, where twenty-five of my stories have gone through the magazine's rigorous fact-checking process.

Between 1996 and 2004, I published four bestsellers about the Kennedys, all of which were well received by the media. I was welcomed on some of the broadcast networks' most highly rated shows (*Today*, *Good Morning America*, and *The View*), interviewed by Charlie Rose, and reviewed by the *New York Times*, *People*, and other popular magazines.

In fact, it wasn't until 2005, when I started writing about Hillary, that I ran into trouble with the media. The *New York Times* assigned Joe Queenan, a self-professed "clown" and negative-styled humorist, to review my first Hillary book, *The Truth about Hillary*. The website Salon describes Queenan as follows: "He has made his living being mean in the pages of *GQ, Movieline, Spy, The New York Times* and countless other publications. He's a self-proclaimed 'full time son of a bitch' who has 'never deviated from [his] chosen career as a sneering churl.'" In his *Times* review of my book, Queenan accused me of calling Hillary a lesbian, which was demonstrably untrue as any fair reading of the book would show. Nonetheless, Queenan's canard has been used by subsequent critics to call my reporting into question.

The *Guardian* assigned Jon Swaine, who reportedly worked for a private intelligence firm with close links to MI6, Britain's foreign intelligence service, to write about *Blood Feud*. Swaine did his investigative best to drag me through the mud, but all he could come up with was that during the divorce from my first wife, I was awarded custody of my two children.

Altogether, I have written five books dealing with Hillary, including the one you are holding in your hands. I have been black-balled by all the major television networks, which, I am told, are frequently warned by the Clinton Slime Room that they will lose their precious access to Hillary if they feature her critics as guests.

My books about Hillary are full of exclusive interviews and news-breaking stories that other journalists have found hard to match. Reporters hate to be scooped, and their envy and jealousy may explain in part why they have parroted the Clinton Slime Room's slander that I make stuff up.

For proof that I don't, let's go to the videotape.

The Truth about Hillary (2005)

In this book, I became the first journalist to explore the source of Hillary's famous pugnacious temperament, which has become an issue in the 2016 presidential race.

I interviewed her first steady boyfriend, Jim Yrigoyen, who at the time of the interview was a high school guidance counselor in Lake Zurich, Illinois. Jim told me the story of being ordered by Hillary to guard a warren of baby rabbits, and not give any of them away to neighborhood boys, no matter how much they begged. Jim readily agreed, but when Hillary's next-door neighbor asked for just one rabbit, Jim couldn't refuse.

"Hillary immediately counted the rabbits," Jim recalled in our interview. "She knew exactly how many she had. She looked at me with disdain and said, 'Did you do this?' When I admitted I did, she...yelled, 'Jim, I trusted you! You big jerk!' Then, she hauled off and punched me in the nose. I was stunned. I reached up and found my nose was bleeding a lot. She had really hurt me."

Also in *The Truth about Hillary*, I was the first journalist to explore the source of Hillary's radical politics, which is also an issue in this year's campaign.

I interviewed the Reverend Don Jones, Hillary's youth minister at the Park Ridge United Methodist Church, who would eventually be fired by his congregation for his "socialist" views. Jones was a major influence in Hillary's early political thinking, and as a high school graduation present, he gave her a subscription to *motive*, a church publication aimed at college students.

Marxist writers were featured in the pages of *motive*. Renegade priest Daniel Berrigan contributed anti–Vietnam War poems. Nat Hentoff defended student militancy. Convicted cop killer Huey Newton was lauded as a victim and visionary. Advice was dispensed on draft-dodging, desertion, and flight to Canada and Sweden.

According to the Methodist Church's archives, to which I had exclusive access, during the 1960s and 1970s *motive* espoused "highly politicized, leftwing ideology, which favored Cuba, socialism, the Black Panthers, and Students for a Democratic Society." In 1972, the last year of its publication, *motive* devoted an entire issue to a radical lesbian/feminist theme, which emphasized the need to destroy "our sexist, racist, capitalist, imperialist system."

"I remember when years later Hillary asked me to come to the White House to counsel her about the Monica Lewinsky matter," recalled the Reverend Don Jones, "and she showed me that she had kept every copy of *motive* magazine. She had read each magazine from cover to cover, and carefully saved each one." And that was in 1998!

The Amateur (2012)

I was the first journalist to interview the Reverend Jeremiah Wright about Barack Obama's ambivalent attitude toward Islam and Christianity, which is also of interest in this presidential year.

My interview with Wright, who, at seventy years of age, was retired from the pulpit of Trinity United Church of Christ, took place on a bleak November morning in his office on the campus of Kwame Nkrumah Academy, a charter school that is named after the late Marxist dictator of the West African nation of Ghana.

"After Barack and I got to know each other, it got to the point where he would just drop by my church to talk," Wright told me. "And the talk gradually moved away from his community organizing concerns—street cleaning, housing, child care, and those kinds of needs—to larger things, more personal things. Like trying to make sense of the world. Like trying to make sense out of the diverse racial and religious background from which he came. He was confused. He wanted to know who he was.

"And I told him, 'Well, you already know the Muslim piece of your background. You studied Islam, didn't you?' And Barack said,

'Yeah, Rev, I studied Islam. But help me understand Christianity, because I already know Islam.' And I said, 'Well, let's start from the beginning. Who do you say Jesus is? Let's boil it down to the basics.'"

"Did you convert Obama from Islam to Christianity?" I asked Wright.

"That's hard to tell," Wright replied. "I think I convinced him that it was okay for him to make a choice in terms of who he believed Jesus is. And I told him it was really okay and not a putdown of the Muslim part of his family or his Muslim friends."

The entire interview was tape recorded, but it was never played on ABC, NBC, CBS, CNN, or NPR. Fox News' *Hannity* was the only TV show that invited me to appear and play the interview.

Blood Feud (2014)

I was the first journalist to break the story of what Hillary knew about the attack on the U.S. consulate in Benghazi and when she knew it—yet another topic of current concern in the presidential race.

In the early hours following the initial alert from the State Department's Operation Center, Cheryl Mills, Hillary's chief of staff, remained at her desk, closely following the battle raging in Benghazi and keeping Hillary updated.

At 8:00 that night, Hillary asked Mills to arrange a conference call with Gregory Hicks, the State Department's deputy chief of mission and chargé d'affaires in the Libyan capital of Tripoli. Hillary and her entire senior staff, including A. Elizabeth "Beth" Jones, the acting assistant secretary of state for Near Eastern Affairs, were on the phone when Hicks said that Ambassador

Christopher Stevens was at a Benghazi hospital and presumed dead. His body could not be recovered, because the al-Qaeda–linked Ansar al-Sharia militia that had mounted the consular attack had surrounded the hospital.

(During the conference call, Hicks mentioned nothing about an anti-Muslim video or a spontaneous protest demonstration. "We saw no demonstrations related to the video anywhere in Libya," Hicks remarked at a later time. And the day after the attack, Assistant Secretary Beth Jones would send out an email saying that Ansar al-Sharia was behind the attack on the American mission.)

Shortly before 10:00 on the night of the attack, Mills told Hillary to expect a call from President Obama. By then, Hillary was one of the most thoroughly briefed officials in Washington on the unfolding disaster in Benghazi. She had no doubt that al-Qaeda had launched a terrorist attack against Americans on the anniversary of 9/11.

"Hillary was stunned when she heard the president talk about the Benghazi attack," according to a member of her team of legal advisers. "Obama wanted her to say that the attack had been a spontaneous demonstration triggered by the video."

After her conversation with Obama, Hillary called Bill Clinton, who was in Little Rock, and told him what Obama wanted her to do. He advised her to go along with the president, and at 10:30 she put out a statement blaming the attack on "inflammatory material posted on the Internet."

Unlikeable (2015)

According to a high-ranking State Department official, Secretary of State John Kerry let Hillary know on the QT that Valerie

Jarrett was out to sabotage her campaign for the White House. Kerry said Jarrett had ordered investigators to do a thorough review of Hillary's State Department papers, and the investigators were also interviewing Foreign Service officers in a hunt for incriminating evidence against Hillary.

The Obamas were bitter rivals of the Clintons and invited Bill and Hillary to dine at the White House only once during Obama's first term in office. The Clintons had a fifth column of friends in the media who kept them up to date on the Obamas' machinations and confirmed what Kerry had told Hillary.

"My contacts and friends in newspapers and TV tell me that they've been contacted by the White House and offered all kinds of negative stories about us," one of Bill's friends quoted him as saying, cautioning that he was paraphrasing the former president. "The Obamas are behind the e-mail story, and they're spreading rumors that I've been with women, that while Hillary was at the State Department she promoted the interests of people and countries who'd done favors for our foundation, and that John Kerry had to clean up the diplomatic messes Hillary left behind."

■■■

Many of the people who told me these stories spoke on the condition of anonymity. This gave the Clinton Slime Room—and its parrots in the mainstream media—the opportunity to call into question the veracity of the stories.

But all contemporary political books use information from anonymous sources to tell important stories that otherwise would go unreported. Bob Woodward, an icon of American journalism, uses unnamed sources both in his reporting for the *Washington Post* and in his books. So do John Heilemann and Mark Halperin, who have used *only* anonymous sources in their two *Game Change* books.

"There has always been doubt about unnamed sources," said Woodward, "and there should be. But you're not going to sit down with people who are in sensitive positions and say, 'I'd like to talk on the record.' They'll say, 'Were you born yesterday?' It just is not going to happen."

Two years ago, Bloomberg News, whose reporting guide strongly discourages the use of unnamed sources, hired Heilemann and Halperin, reportedly paying each of them $1 million a year.

"Why do journalists use anonymous sources?" wrote Kurt Andersen in *New York Magazine*. "Because people who are willing to tell reporters interesting things—that is, confidential or disturbing information or opinions—are usually disinclined to appear to be the candid plain talkers or snitches or whistle-blowers or gossips or backstabbers they are."

If that doesn't shut up the Clinton Slime Room, I don't know what will.

—Edward Klein
New York City
September 2016